RAISING MONEY FOR CHURCH BUILDING PROJECTS

RAISING MONEY FOR CHURCH BUILDING PROJECTS

Arthur W. Lumley

ABINGDON PRESS

New York   Nashville

RAISING MONEY FOR CHURCH BUILDING PROJECTS

Copyright MCMLIV by Pierce & Washabaugh

Library of Congress Catalog Card Number: 54-8240

SET UP, PRINTED, AND BOUND BY THE PARTHENON PRESS, AT NASHVILLE, TENNESSEE, UNITED STATES OF AMERICA

To the memory of
CHARLES A. TEVEBAUGH

Lawyer, Y.M.C.A. state secretary, U.S.O. director,
expert fund raiser, loyal churchman,
good friend, and wise counselor

FOREWORD

Sooner or later every church undertakes a building project that calls for more money than can be supplied in its regular budget. If the church is new, it must buy a lot and erect a complete plant, either all at one time or in stages. If the church is already housed, growth in membership demands a larger sanctuary, educational building, or recreational facilities —or perhaps a new home for the pastor. Even a church with declining membership finds its old building in need of replacement, modernization, or major repair—or perhaps the paying off of a mortgage that has hampered progress—and a community survey may show that rebuilding on a new site will reverse the decline and start the congregation off on a new growth.

Whatever the building project, if it is sizable, there is only one satisfactory way to provide the funds—put on a well-planned, well-manned, well-organized campaign for pledges.

The plan for a fund-raising campaign described in these pages is a fairly simple procedure designed for the church where the canvass is to be directed and carried out by members of the congregation. The large church, with a substantial amount to raise, will do well to bring in an experienced campaign director from the denominational headquarters, or else to employ one of the several independent companies that specialize in directing the financial campaigns of churches and similar organizations. A much larger amount will usually result from such skilled guidance. Where a church cannot or will not employ professional help, however, the leaders among its own membership can often achieve a high degree of success by using the techniques which experienced campaign directors have proved to be most effective.

The general pattern for a successful fund-raising campaign has been established through a half century of experimentation by unnumbered campaign organizers in churches of all sorts across the nation. But every director has his own ideas about specific details. The plan described here draws on many years of observation and experience, and it is made up entirely of methods that have worked successfully in practice. Yet this is not to suggest that everything in this plan is the one and only way to do it in every church. Some procedures may not be necessary in certain situations, and various modifications may be wise to fit local circumstances. The campaign director and his committee should choose whatever will fit the church, the project at hand, and above all the preferences of the workers and contributors whose enthusiastic co-operation is the indispensable element in every fund-raising campaign.

ARTHUR W. LUMLEY

CONTENTS

THREE
VITAL
QUESTIONS

1

Your church is planning a major building project. This is a critical period in its life, for its future growth—in numbers, in influence, and in Christian service to the community—depends on achieving the goal.

At such a time your church needs money, of course. But it needs much more. Imagine that some wealthy person in your community should suddenly give the church all the money required for the project. Would that alone accomplish what you envision? Rather the whole congregation must develop a spirit of loyalty and sacrificial devotion, and must unite in determination to make the fullest possible use of the new facilities for the glory of God and the service of men.

The one best way to gain both financial and spiritual objectives is to put on a campaign—which means a well-planned, intensive effort to see every member and friend of the church and get his pledge to the building fund. It has been demonstrated over and over again that the right kind of fund-raising drive will meet both needs. The two things interact: a spirit of devotion inspires generous giving, and the act of giving increases the spirit of devotion.

Here's an example that shows how this principle operates in a financial campaign that has spiritual foundations. A small congregation had "swarmed" from the parent church in a midwestern city and was meeting in rented quarters. There was a modest growth during the next two years. After that it became evident that the group had reached its limit, both in numbers and in interest. The members must either secure an acceptable site and put up a building or gradually fade out of the picture.

Committees were appointed, and innumerable meetings were held. Prayer for guidance was central in all the sessions. All facets of the problem were discussed before the congregation almost every Sunday morning for several months. At first the outlook seemed to be hopeless, but there was a developing spirit of devotion and determination in the group that could not be denied. The members were bound and bent on going forward. Not for one instant was there any thought of turning back. No defeatist voice was heard from any member of the congregation during this time when vague hopes and dreams slowly crystallized into action.

Eventually some long-range planning was done. Very early in this period the denominational headquarters was asked for help, and a field representative was sent to the church. His statement to the official board, after a survey of the situation, was so searching as to be well remembered to this day.

"As board members of your church," he said in substance, "you must be fully aware of what you are trying to do. Your congregation is small, and there are no wealthy members. Only if you are willing to work together, and to undergo any sacrifice, will you succeed. As board members you must lead the way. Some of you may be planning to buy a new car; you'll have to give it up. Some of you may intend to build a new house; you must give that up, too. New cars and new houses may come later, but for the immediate future you must forgo them to build a church. It's going to require deep personal sacrifice. The price is high. Do you think you can pay it? Can you see your way through to the end?"

After a moment of stunned silence one of the church officials replied: "No, we can't see our way through to the end. The money is not in sight, and we don't know where it is. But we have asked for guidance, and we believe firmly that we have had our answer. We are determined to venture forth in faith that this thing—which, humanly speaking, seems impossible—can be accomplished."

This wise counselor was probing deep into the heart of the church, and his meaning was clear, keen, and revealing. He was concerned about money, but even more about the spirit in which the group should undertake its task.

Following his visit a building site was selected, and a survey and church census carried on in the neighborhood confirmed that it was well located. A consulting church architect was called in for conference, and preliminary sketches and floor plans of the proposed new building were presented for the consideration of the building committee. A short time later, definite plans were made for the initial campaign.

The campaign was carefully mapped out and carried through with efficiency. The members pledged generously, but with their limited numbers could raise only 85 per cent of the cost of the site. Nevertheless enthusiasm was kept up, and a second campaign a year later completed payment on the site and raised a third of the amount needed for the new building. The following year a third campaign brought in half the balance needed and made it possible to secure a loan for the rest. As the church building began to rise, the community started taking notice. People came to visit, liked the atmosphere of friendliness and sincere devotion, and decided to be members. After two years the time seemed ripe to build a parsonage, and a fourth campaign was put on.

Now, after six years, the congregation has its complete buildings and grounds, and is growing almost too fast for its own good. There is a moderately heavy debt, but it has been carried by the congregation without undue strain. Paralleling a marked increase in membership have come other benefits—a deepening of the spiritual life of the church, a sense of community responsibility, and a keen interest in world missions. There has been a discernible carry-over from the battles fought and victories won into the present life of the congregation.

In comparison with the spirit which prompted this congregation to undertake and carry through such an ambitious building program the financial element seems almost incidental. As a result of what had gone before, the money came in sufficient volume to finance the project. This is not to say that the money-raising task was easy. There were days of doubt, discouragement, and uncertainty. It was hard—almost beyond description at times. But it was done, and done successfully, because a group of people believed strongly enough that it could be done and should be done, and were willing under God's leading to undertake it.

What are the elements that made this project successful? Chiefly these: constant and continued prayer for guidance; invincible determination, combined with willingness to work and to sacrifice; united and enthusiastic congregation; careful planning, with the help of the best counsel from experts that could be secured; and sacrificial giving by the members and friends of the church. The implications are plain for any church official responsible for leadership in a major building project.

In contrast to this example consider the story told by one who happened to visit the opening workers' dinner of a campaign in a large church seeking to raise a substantial amount for a new building. Scarcely had the meal been finished, he reported, when one of the "generals" rose to state with indignation that he had been let down. He had been assured, he declared, that someone would recruit a set of captains and teams for his division and that he would then oversee their work. But no one had done anything about it, and here he was at the kickoff of active solicitation with his whole division nonexistent.

Soon after he sat down, someone else got up to add to the gloom by observing: "This is not a good time to raise money. The campaign is ill advised and should be put off till next year." By this time everyone's spirits were down around zero, and it looked as if any further bit of wet-blanket oratory might well scuttle the whole undertaking. But the worst was yet to come when it came to light that no adequate plan had been made for distribution of the prospect cards to the workers.

The meeting broke up in confusion, with a sense of impending failure already in the air. The workers were licked before they started, and could secure less than a third of their goal. The final result was a series of excuses, recriminations, and broken friendships.

Without knowing all that led up to this fiasco, we can see plainly the reasons for it—not only an inexcusable lack of wise planning and careful preparations, but an even more serious lack of unity, determination, and devotion. The factors that made for success in the first example are almost totally lacking here.

Because conducting a successful building-fund campaign involves so much more than mere efficient methods of promotion and solicitation, church leaders ought never to think of planning such a drive till they have made sure that the necessary foundations for it have been laid. To make sure, they should investigate and get right answers to three questions.

Is this project a sound investment?

The leaders must be convinced themselves that it is sound if they are to enter into it with wholehearted enthusiasm and be able to kindle the same spirit in the minds and hearts of the soliciting organization. They must have a deep conviction that the cause is a worthy one and that the sacrifices of the members will be more than repaid by continuing material and spiritual benefits to the congregation and to the community. Only with this motivation will the members of the group throw themselves into the struggle with abandon and see it through to the end.

The chairman and his committee will therefore examine the project before the church with great care and analyze it thoroughly. Will the completion of this project meet present needs? Will it take its place in a soundly conceived, long-range plan that will satisfy the needs of future years—ten years, twenty years, later? The planning that has been done, or will now be done, must satisfy the committee that the project is completely sound, not only in its component parts but in its total aspect.

The location of the building is of vital importance. It is a tragic error to put a church in the wrong place. Our cities are dotted with such blunders, even to the point of a half-dozen churches in as many adjacent blocks. No effort should be spared to get the best available counsel on the subject, based on whatever studies, techniques, and processes may be required. The church building is going to be there for a long time, and its future is at stake.

In one case a church building was located right on the border of the largest cemetery in the city. Several square miles which would normally be filled with homes are occupied only by the dead, and a large area from which the church would draw under happier conditions can contribute nothing, either in personnel or in finance. This example—and there are many others like it across the country—points up the need for a thorough examination of all the factors in the case before a building site is chosen.

In his book *Church Work in the City,* Frederick A. Shippey

lists six guiding principles in the establishment of a new church: (1) a concentration of unchurched Protestant people, (2) freedom from physical and psychological barriers, (3) freedom from unwholesome or hobbling competition, (4) a conspicuous, accessible site, (5) an adequate plant, and (6) an effective ministry.

A religious census is needed to show the number of unchurched Protestant people within a reasonable distance of the proposed location. This will list the number of adults, with their church preference, and the number and ages of the children.

A survey of the neighborhood is also needed. This will spot any barriers to future growth, such as rivers, ravines, railroads, cemeteries, and factories. These all reduce the space which can be used for home building. It will also show the number of Protestant churches already in the community, some of which might cause costly competition. Finally the report will deal with traffic problems and parking facilities, both of which have an important bearing on the "conspicuous, accessible site" mentioned by Shippey. The denominational headquarters will be able to furnish advice about this survey —and perhaps send a field man to help with it.

Off-the-street parking has become a necessity in many cities in recent years. This is not only for the convenience of the parishioners but for the peace of mind of the nearby home owners, who do not appreciate having cars parked in front of their houses or in their driveways. Some cities have ordinances requiring parking lots for churches and other organizations, and prescribe the size.

The new site must be big enough for later development, particularly if the structure is to be built unit by unit. The deed to the property must be examined to see that required setbacks from the lot lines do not cramp the space needed for building. It goes without saying that a good attorney should pass on the abstract.

Very early in the planning it is wise to consult the comity committee of the local council of churches—or if there is no council of churches, whatever committee from the ministers' association or other local organization is acting as a clearinghouse on the subject. This body may already have the desired information from previous surveys of the neighborhood, or several neighborhoods, which are under consideration, and thus save considerable time and effort. Information about any other churches which may be looking over the same area may also be had.

The object of such an organization, of course, is to spot new churches in favorable locations, to space them so that unchurched sections may be served, and to prevent excessive competition where churches are located too close to one another. The leaders of a new church will wish to co-operate in this purpose as well as to secure information.

The foregoing paragraphs apply particularly to the new congregation which is seeking a good building site. But they apply also to the established congregation where rebuilding is in prospect. The old location must not be taken for granted. A neighborhood survey may prove that it would be an advantage to move to a new site. The advent of apartment and rooming houses, the encroachment of business and industrial concerns, the gradual moving in of other races or nationalities—all these changes may show the wisdom of moving to a more promising section of the city. Otherwise the neighborhood changes may result in a reduction in attendance at services and a loss in membership, with eventually a drop in current income for the operation of the church program and for retirement of the debt on the new building. Even if the present neighborhood has not yet started to decline, a survey may show that in a new neighborhood opportunities for wider service and faster growth would far overweigh the cost of the move.

The same may be said of the old congregation which is planning a remodeling program. Is it wise to remain in this location? Is the neighborhood such as will be served by the kind of program which this church provides? Is there any evidence that future growth in the membership may be anticipated, or, on the other hand, will the church in time reach a point when an inevitable decline will set in? Can adjoining land be bought for more parking space or, should they be needed, for more buildings or an enlargement of the present structure?

All these questions, and many others, will be answered by putting on a well-conducted neighborhood survey and church census; and this essential information can be secured in no other way.

The size of the building is of equally vital importance. Naturally consideration of it will take into account all the facts about present membership and attendance. But here again wise planning for the future must be based on the sort of information provided by a neighborhood survey and census. What about the population trends in the locality? What about the number of Protestant families? What estimate can be made of the probable growth in members? What are the needs, as nearly as they can be forecast, over the next several decades?

No one should minimize the difficulty of answering these questions. But the attempt must be made in the light of all the information that can be secured. Supplying merely the immediate needs will prove to be a short-sighted policy which will be keenly regretted later. It's the total picture that must be taken into account.

For instance, what size should the sanctuary be? Years ago many were built too large, leaving a bigger burden of debt than the congregation could carry. Your church architect will tell you to estimate your probable membership in the years ahead and build a sanctuary to hold about one third of them. Social rooms or parlors in the rear may be opened to care for the overflow at Christmas and Easter. Or multiple services may be held on Sunday mornings, as many churches are now doing. It's safe to say that the average pastor would rather preach in a smaller, well-filled sanctuary than in a larger one that's half empty.

On the other hand, if the church is located favorably in a growing community, it would make a serious mistake in building for its present congregation only, simply because it couldn't raise enough money for something larger. Much of its investment would be lost if the building soon became overcrowded and the membership ceased to increase.

Whether *the plan of the building* is such as to meet the needs of the congregation is a question of obvious importance, but it is surprising how many building committees—and even architects who keep up to date in other fields—plan a new church on the basis of sentimental recollections of their childhood.

In architectural design and equipment the modern sanctuary is a far cry from the old auditorium built fifty years ago. The concert-hall atmosphere is gone. The emphasis is on design and arrangement—as well as seating, lighting, ventilating, acoustics, and general decor—that will combine in beauty and quiet dignity to inspire a spirit of reverence and devotion. Most churches have found that worshipers are no longer inspired by gazing at an ornate pulpit stand, a garish display of choir singers, and an imposing bank of gilded organ pipes. Instead they seek to focus attention on the divine rather than the human, designing the whole chancel so that every element will contribute to this end. Increasing numbers now prefer the divided chancel, with lectern and pulpit on opposite sides, the choir unobtrusively seated behind them, and an altar, Communion table, or other center of worship in the middle, its effect accentuated by skillful lighting.

Much to improve the worshipful atmosphere of a sanctuary can be done in a remodeling program. The old auditorium can be given a "face lifting." Under competent architectural advice, with a rearrangement of the floor space, new seating, new lighting, and other modern features, it can be transformed into a place of worship—a "sanctuary" in the best sense of the word.

Making over the antiquated educational factilities in most old churches is a tough problem. It's enough to tax the best brains in the architectural profession. But it has been done successfully, even where the outlook seemed to be hopeless. This observer once visited a congregation of three hundred families at the Sunday-school hour. The adults were using the auditorium for their classes, the young people were in curtained recesses at the back of the balcony, while the small fry were sent to the "basement"—a term that should be expunged from all church terminology. This section had never been finished although the building was fifty years old. The classrooms were small, cold (it was late fall), dark, and undecorated. The walls were unpainted brick partitions, and the corridors were channels cut through mounds of exposed earth. And yet in these surroundings little children were supposed to be learning to give religion first place in their lives.

Two years later the place was completely changed. New leadership had come into the church, funds were raised, and extensive improvements were made. Bright and cheerful classrooms, well furnished and well lighted, replaced the dingy cubbyholes that had existed before. Unhappily the smaller children were still sent to the remodeled basement, but a vigorous young church board was bent on a complete rehabilitation program, including a new sanctuary and an educational building.

New teaching methods have brought marked changes in architectural design and equipment for church classrooms. Not so many years ago the child could do little but sit and listen (few did) and squirm. More effective methods in education are gradually altering such outmoded practices. It is recognized that children "learn what they do," so classrooms must be large enough to allow dramatizations of Bible stories, the making of relief maps of Palestine, and a thousand and one similar activities. The children now teach themselves, in a sense, while the teacher simply sets the stage.

The experienced church architect knows all about these new techniques. He has the answer. But, in addition, it will be wise for the building committee to get full information from the educational board of the denomination.

Ample space for social and recreational facilities must not be forgotten. And the dining room and kitchen are most important adjuncts to the church in this modern day. Special attention must be given to the kitchen. It must be large enough and furnished with tubs, sinks, water heaters, refrigerators, pots, pans, kettles, and all the other equipment necessary to serve the needs of the congregation. So many church events are now held around the dinner tables and the never-ending task is so onerous for the women of the congregation that it is only fair to the cooks and servers to supply them with the best available equipment.

Careful planning is needed for the new parsonage. In the natural course of events the pastor's family may increase in size, and allowances must be made. Here's a case in point: A newly married minister and his wife came to a small city church. A parsonage with three bedrooms, two bathrooms, and a study was built for them a year later at a cost of $27,500—after some debate over whether a smaller house would not serve. Now there are two children in the family circle, and in time the pastor may be forced to give up his study and prepare his sermons in the church. The building committee had planned wisely in providing a building as large as this. Had they been more conservative, it would have resulted in hardship for the family and embarrassment for the church.

The location of the parsonage is another important question. It used to be taken for granted that it would be built next to the church. But not any more. It was altogether too handy—for things to be borrowed and the living room to be appropriated for an overflowing class on Sunday mornings. Ministers and their families appreciate the blessings of privacy just as other people do, and the present-day parsonage location is a block or two away, at least, and sometimes several miles.

Is the congregation informed and favorable?

The campaign chairman and his committee will be greatly concerned over the attitude of the members, who must supply the money. If they know what is going on and like it, the plan will have a good chance to succeed. If they do not, there isn't a ghost of a chance.

The outline of the project will not come full-blown into being all at once. It will be considered and discussed for a long time before it emerges in concrete form. The members must be fully conscious of what is happening at all times, and in those denominations where it is necessary formal congregational approval should be asked as the more important steps are taken.

Differences of opinion will inevitably exist. Some will favor a modernization program because they think it will cost less, while others will insist that the old building be razed and a new one put up in its place. Some will feel that the old classrooms and departments can be made over, while others will declare a new educational building is an absolute necessity. If it's a new building on a new site, ideas will differ on its location on the lot, on the size and shape of the sanctuary, the location of the kitchen and dining room, the kinds of recreational facilities to be provided, whether to use bricks, stone, or cement blocks for the outer walls, and a multitude of other items.

Experience has shown that these differences can be resolved by careful handling. The services of the consulting architect will be of inestimable value at this point. Out of his background of information on what has been done in other places will come tactful recommendations as to what should be done here. Few reasonable people will challenge the opinions of the expert, and even the apparently irreconcilable rebel will usually adjust to the situation.

But progress must be made slowly. Here's what happened when every rule in the book was violated: In one case a modernization program was planned by the building committee and a campaign for funds started with little preparation. No church architect was brought in for consultation and the congregation was poorly informed and had literally nothing to say about the undertaking. Severe criticism came from several of the older members, former leaders in the church, who had not been consulted. Each of them had a considerable following, resulting in a formidable body of opposition. As the canvass proceeded, it was found that at least 40 per cent of the members were against the undertaking and refused to contribute. Needless to say, the effort failed.

The congregation must be informed at every turn, and opportunity for questions and full discussion must be afforded. This must be done even where some constitutent body has been given power to act. A campaign for money needs a harmonious and enthusiastic effort on the part of every group and individual. Extraordinary care on this point may save a lot of grief later.

As vague outlines of the project begin to take shape in the early months, the routine procedure might be along the following lines:

1. Preliminary discussion by the board
2. General presentation to the congregation
3. Appointment of a building committee
4. Consultation with the local council of churches
5. Visits from denominational field men
6. Study of survey and census and the architect's recommendations to the building committee
7. Building-committee recommendations to the board
8. Board recommendations to the congregation
9. Decision by congregation or other authorized body on course to be followed

This line of action is suggested for the church which is congregational in its form of government. In others, where the local group is not fully autonomous, plans must be presented to authorized supervisory agencies for approval.

The attitude of the congregation will depend in large measure on the kind of project to be undertaken. In some situations the need is obvious and keenly felt by all. Anyone can see that the course which has been chosen is reasonable and right and that it will best serve the interests of the congregation and the community, and the members will rally around and support it to the utmost of their resources. In other circumstances the need may be equally great but less apparent to the average member, and less likely to arouse emotion and enthusiasm. The campaign leaders must take these psychological factors into account.

A new building for a new congregation offers the most thrilling task of all. The job is difficult because the membership is small and the giving capacity limited. The normal growth of the organization is curtailed because it meets in a rented hall or school building where the facilities, both for worship and for Sunday school, are inadequate. The congregation needs a new building to stimulate growth, yet any marked increase in numbers is held back by the lack of good housing. The task is thrilling nevertheless. As time goes on, the members will be more and more dissatisfied with their meeting place; and there will develop a strong desire for a building they can call their own. This attitude will grow stronger and stronger until they will virtually demand of themselves a workable plan for the purchase of a building site and the financing of a new church plant.

An established congregation which should move confronts the campaign committee with a more difficult problem. The older congregation has habits of long standing, traditions, family connections, old ties, sentimental attachments, and whatnot to consider when the all-important move to a new location is brought to the fore. A survey of the present neighborhood may provide ample proof of the necessity for the move, but it will take much education to make the results of the survey meaningful to most of the members. Invariably there will be disagreements before the decision is made—and probably after, as well. The planning committee must act with extreme care and over long periods of time so as to bring about as great a degree of harmony as may be possible. Even then there will be those who will remain with the present building, if another denomination takes over, rather than go with the congregation.

The campaign for funds will prove to be more difficult than with the new church. The members of the established congregation do not feel the same sense of urgency and are harder to please; many of them will be less generous in their support. Where persons in the new group are willing to pledge almost beyond their means, the members in the old church are likely to be more conservative, and the average gift from the general membership will be lower. The technique indicated, of course, is a longer period of preparation for the canvass, with a well-worked-out plan for intensive cultivation and promotion.

Rebuilding, remodeling, or enlarging may be harder to finance than an entirely new site and plant. Many of the members will feel that the present structure has served its purpose well, and they are satisfied with what they have. The pattern has been pretty well set through the years, and to arouse certain sections of the congregation from a state of near apathy is not an easy undertaking. But it's not impossible. It has been done, it's being done now, and it can be done again if the people are challenged with the needs and the opportunities.

Burning a mortgage is a necessary goal, and the time when it can be achieved may have a distinct bearing on the future of the church. Plans for regular payments of a building debt should be instituted and carried through. If the progress of the church calls for faster action, a campaign should be undertaken, at the right time, to remove the burden entirely. But this is hard money to raise alone. While conscientious church officials will be concerned about wiping out the obligation, debt retirement is totally lacking in glamour and has little appeal for the general membership. Usually it is better to include the debt in a campaign for a new building or a modernization project on the plea that the church should be free of old obligations before it incurs new ones.

Is the plan for financing practical?

Any church confronted with an improvement or new-building program needs a sound, over-all financial plan based on a long-range view of the organization's future. What will the project cost in dollars and cents? The architect can give a reasonably close estimate after over-all plans are agreed on, and can usually make a rough estimate at earlier stages. On this basis the financing committee must plan how the money may be raised. By one or more special campaigns? By supplementing what is contributed by a loan? How big may the loan be, if one is required, and how will it be repaid? Should the complete building operation be carried through unit by unit, saving some of the more expensive parts of the structure to be financed by a larger membership several years in the future?

The amount of the loan should be within the limit of what the membership can repay in a reasonable time without hindering the program of the church. There have been instances in the past where congregations assumed crippling burdens of debt that they, and their children after them, struggled under for years. This is not done in the present day, for church officials realize that the same good business judgment should prevail in church affairs as is used in their own lines of work.

Church-extension executives have set up a formula for determining a safe loan for a church. Take three factors: (1) 40 per cent of the cost of construction, (2) 3½ times the annual budget, and (3) an amount equal to $200 for each church family. Figure up the total and divide by three to strike an average. This is the answer, according to these church specialists. For example, a church needs $100,000 for its building program, there are 250 families in the membership, and the annual budget is $15,000. Under the formula, this church could safely take on a loan of $47,500, leaving $52,500 to be raised. A reasonable amount should be added to this goal with which to carry the loan.

A good method in retiring the loan is an agreement with the lending agency to pay back 1 per cent a month, including principal and interest. This will liquidate the debt in approximately ten years. After the term of building-fund pledges has run out, it will likely be necessary to include an item in the annual budget to carry interest payments.

Bank officers are not eager to make loans to churches, especially when money is tight. They do not wish to bring pressure to bear in case of delinquent payments; it's not good public relations. Better terms and a more sympathetic response may result from dealing with a church lending agency. Here, too, will be found a group of officials who are conversant with the problems facing the church, and their counsel will be of value.

The amount that can be raised in special campaigns is the question that will be uppermost in the minds of the campaign committee and other financial leaders in the church. While no final and conclusive answer can be given, there are certain recognized formulas which will give some indication of what can be expected.

1. The average church will do well in a one-year campaign (pledges payable over a period of one year) to raise an amount equal to twice the annual budget for current expenses, missions, and benevolences. This will be the top figure in most cases, and it will take several large gifts to reach it. Unless these are in prospect, the expectation should be lower.

2. Officials of one of the big denominations state that in their experience from three to four times the annual budget can be raised for building purposes in a two-year campaign.

3. Since the big pledges will mean the difference between success and failure, a quiet inquiry among board members will reveal what can be expected. These folks must show a high standard for the others. If they don't, the prospects are bad. Apply the following formula and see what happens:

a) Will some board member give 10 per cent of what is needed?

b) Will five board members, including the high man, give 25 per cent?

c) Will twenty-five subscribers (board members and others) give 50 per cent? If they will, it's pretty fair sailing ahead. If they won't, it's going to be rough weather.

Let it be repeated that campaigns for money do not follow

any set pattern. The formulas given here will not apply in all cases, nor will any other. These are but straws in the wind, and pretty frail ones, at that. For instance, one church raised $90,000 with $3,000 as the biggest gift. Another church raised $875,000 with the first half million given by twelve families. There are all kinds of variations from the norm, but when several hundred campaign figures are analyzed, the tabulated averages give something to work on. Professional campaign directors rely on experience tables that group churches into categories according to their age, giving record, predominant type of membership, and so on. With these they are able to forecast rather accurately what any particular church is likely to raise in a well-conducted campaign. Possibly local church officials can secure such information from their denominational headquarters.

Building unit by unit often solves the problem when the total needed is beyond what can be foreseen from a campaign plus a safe loan. Very few congregations entering a promising field are able to finance in one campaign, or even two, the kind of extensive building program which the neighborhood deserves. This is especially true of a new congregation. If the members defer building until all the money needed is in sight, it will mean a delay of several years during which many prospective members will be lost. On the other hand, if they start building too quickly, they will either run into financing trouble or put up buildings too small to meet the needs of the community. The way out of this dilemma is to draw up plans for the total structure that will eventually be needed, and then divide it into units that can be built separately as the membership grows.

A few years ago it was a common sight to see the foundation and basement of a church covered with temporary roofing and used for all purposes for several years till the congregation could raise money to complete the superstructure. This plan is still often followed successfully, but it has the disadvantage that the truncated building is ugly and does not attract new members. Therefore many churches now prefer to plan a building that can be divided into units horizontally, so that the first unit can be entirely completed—at least on the outside—and give visitors as well as members a sample of the beauty of the future total plant. For example, in one recent operation of this sort an experienced church architect planned the educational unit, including a social hall, to be built toward the rear of the site. Classrooms are separated by modern soundproof curtains, which fold back to supply plenty of room for the worship services and social meetings of the present congregation. When the membership has grown larger and more money is in prospect, the sanctuary will be erected in front.

If a unit plan is impracticable, the church with a building project beyond its present means must either cut down on its plans or else postpone starting on them till the prospect is more favorable. Usually it is wiser to postpone action rather than put up a building that will be proved inadequate almost before the mortar has firmly set. In such a situation, to maintain interest, as well as to build up a part of the funds which will be needed when construction begins, the announcement of the opening of a special building-fund account at the bank may be a wise move. It will bring in a number of contributions from certain of the members and from organized groups in the church. Any action toward a program of solicitation, however, should be quiet, informal, and restricted to the inner circle of the membership, so that the edge may not be taken off the highly organized effort to come later.

Whatever is decided upon, there should be elements of Christian faith, daring, and imagination, as well as good business judgment, in the minds and hearts of the people as the project takes form.

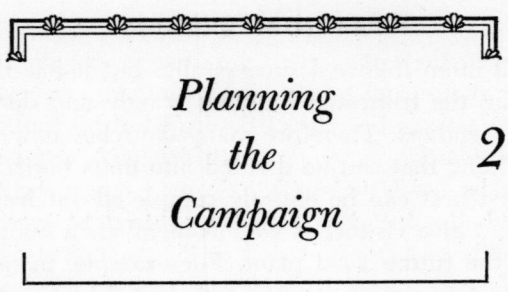

Planning
the
Campaign
2

A fund-raising effort must be thoroughly planned before any work is done on the actual details of the organization. If this course is followed, procedural mistakes will be avoided, and each component part of the operation will fit into its proper place.

When the general plans for the building project and its over-all financing have been well laid, the campaign committee will have a sound basis for determining what must be accomplished by the campaign, as well as the probable response in contributions by the congregation. With such facts and estimates before it the committee must make at the beginning certain basic decisions.

The term of the pledges

Most members and friends will contribute by signing pledges to make regular weekly or monthly payments to the building fund over a certain period of time. This period, or term, is usually set at one, two, or three years—although some church-extension executives recommend a maximum of two years. Choosing the right term may have great bearing on the success of the campaign and the project.

If it appears that the members can pay the amount needed

within a year, there is obviously no use in dragging the thing out longer. Simply set to work on a campaign that will arouse everyone to assume his part of the load for this limited period. The funds raised by a single campaign with a one-year term may often be combined with a loan to cover the total cost. If so, it is better to take on a reasonable debt, which can be paid off with amounts included in the annual budget over a number of years, rather than to strain for an objective clearly out of reach or to stretch out the term and thus delay construction of a building needed for the church's progress.

On the other hand, if it appears that, even counting on a safe loan, more money than the congregation can pay in one year is called for, then a choice must be made. Is it better to put on a single campaign for two- or three-year pledges, or two or more successive campaigns for one-year pledges? The choice depends on the local situation.

Here are the advantages of a single long-term campaign:

1. The job, if successful, is finished at one time; and workers can devote their efforts to other needed activities.

2. Campaign expenses (printing, postage, meals, extra secretarial help, and so on) are incurred only once.

3. Workers and members in general can be aroused to a peak of enthusiasm not likely to be repeated.

4. Members will get in the habit of generous giving to the church and at the end of the term may be willing to transfer their support to an enlarged program or some missionary or benevolent cause.

5. The psychological atmosphere of the church may be better, through freedom from worry or pressure.

In contrast the plan of repeated one-year campaigns has these advantages:

1. The church is tied to one pattern for only a short time. If economic or other conditions change, it can more easily adjust to the differences.

2. If the goal is not reached, the church's hands are not tied for so long. The members have the tacit assurance that they will not be solicited again during the life of the pledges they have signed, when any further appeal is likely to cause resentment. If the pledges cover only one year, another chance to reach the goal comes quickly.

3. New members, who would otherwise make little or no contribution to the building fund, are pledged in the later drives.

4. Shrinkage from cancellations, removals, and deaths will be much less during a short term.

5. The ideal of stewardship and the importance of the church activities represented by the building project are continuously emphasized to the congregation.

In general the plan of repeated campaigns with a one-year term seems better for the newly organized congregation which looks forward to its first building operation. Enthusiasm is likely to be at white heat, and the members will stand for two, or even three, campaigns. For example, a new congregation of 140 members, which had been meeting in rented quarters for several years, needed a large sum for a new building; the very life of the church depended on it. Knowing that the full amount could not be raised in one canvass, the congregation decided to take as large a bite of the total as possible. The resulting campaign on a one-year basis was successful. The members went out again fifteen months later and got almost as much in cash and pledges as they did the first time. These two efforts, plus as large a loan as it was safe to assume, financed the new structure. The debt is now being reduced regularly and rather easily by the growing congregation.

On the other hand most older congregations will do better with a single campaign for two- or three-year pledges. The members usually will not submit to multiple campaigns, and it will be hard enough to get up momentum for one effort, let alone two or three.

Along with the matter of the term comes the question of whether weekly or monthly payments should be indicated on the pledge cards, as well as in promotional materials. A few years ago it was the usual practice to ask the contributor to put down on the card the total amount that he would pay during the life of the pledge. In the present day, however, the emphasis is placed on a weekly or monthly payment plan—for good psychological reasons. An amount of ten dollars a week or forty a month will not seem such a drain on the prospect as a lump sum of five hundred dollars in a year's time, although the smaller payments will add up to about the same total in each case. The weekly payment plan is preferable in most situations because (1) the contributor is accustomed to paying on this basis to the current budget and (2) the unit of payment is smaller and seems less burdensome. Of course in the last analysis the contributor is the judge not only of how much he will pay but of how he will pay it. Nevertheless through publicity materials and also the form in which the pledge card is made out, the attention of the prospect is drawn to either the weekly or the monthly plan; and he is more likely to pledge generously if the suggested method of payment seems easy to him.

The committee must decide on these two questions, the term of the pledges and weekly or monthly payments, as early in the planning period as possible. The pledge cards can't be printed until they are settled, and the cards will be needed by the office secretary in making up the mailing list in the very first days of the preparatory stage. Also the building-fund envelopes must be ordered at this time so that delivery may be made well before the solicitation begins. The number of envelopes needed in each carton will depend on the term of the pledges and on whether payments are to be expected on a weekly or monthly basis. For instance, if pledges are to run for one year and be paid weekly, each contributor will require fifty-two envelopes. The committee will be wise to order more cartons of envelopes than they think will be needed, since the added cost of a few dozen more will be negligible.

The campaign goal

The goal announced for any effort to raise money has an important psychological effect. Setting the right amount is often a baffling question, however. It should be large enough to present a strong challenge to the congregation but not so large as to discourage the team workers. No set rule will apply as so many factors enter in—the age of the church, the character of the membership, its sacrificial spirit, its education and training in the practice of stewardship, and the expertness with which the canvass is prepared for and carried through.

The truth is that few churches have the faintest idea what they can raise unless they have had campaigns for capital money in recent years. One classic example is the church board which was sure that it could raise a large sum because it had put on no campaign, except for the current budget, for forty-seven years. The reasoning was simple—the congregation had given little, so now it would be in a good mood to give much. Nothing could be further from the truth; it works just the other way. No spirit of stewardship had been built up in this group. They hadn't acquired the habit of sharing, and they didn't know how to give. This was amply demonstrated in the later campaign.

Be sure of this: a high but attainable goal will bring in more money than an unreachable one. If a church raises $50,000 on a $60,000 goal by the closing night of the campaign, the workers will be willing to continue for another week, recanvass their bigger givers, increase their own pledges, and go beyond the figure which had been set. And they'll have a royal good time doing it. But if they raise $50,000 on a goal of $100,000, they will quit right there. What's the use? They're licked, and they know it.

Such a failure is bad for a church. It's habit-forming. Conversely a victory, even after the hardest kind of struggle, kindles and fires the spirit and life of the group. They'll be more ready to tackle the next challenge that comes along.

It is apparent that the goal must be considered in relation to the length of the term over which pledges are to run. Obviously more money will result from payments over three years than a one-year term will produce, but the committee must take into account certain of the disadvantages that go with the three-year plan. With these factors in mind the committee may find some help from a re-examination of the formulas which appear in Chapter 1. The points to be considered might be summed up as follow:

1. The total amount needed
2. The size of the loan that the church can carry
3. Whether more than one campaign will be needed
4. The term of the pledges
5. The giving potential of the congregation, based on current budget contributions
6. A private inquiry among the number of the big givers (or a conservative estimate of what they will give)

In calculating the amount needed a modest campaign budget must be included. It's a well-known principle that it takes money to make money. It's equally true that it takes money to raise money. Too much saving at this point may mean decreased campaign results. A sample budget for a $30,000 to $50,000 goal will be about as follows:

Printing	$250
Postage	50
Office supplies	50
Dinners	200
Extra office help	50
Contingencies	50
	$650

Promotional strategy

Good promotion and publicity are essential to the success of any fund-raising campaign. It must be well planned, unified, and timed so that every segment of the membership feels the impact not only once but again and again. All the planning should be around some phase of the central theme and purpose of the effort.

A name for the campaign will be needed in all the publicity, and it ought to be as attractive and eye-catching as possible. If it can convey the intent and purpose of the canvass, all the better. The following have been used, time and time again: Anniversary Campaign, Memorial Campaign, New Building Campaign, Building Fund Campaign, Educational Building Campaign, Church Enlargement Campaign, Church Modernization Campaign, and Fellowship Campaign. None of these is particularly distinctive, and it may be that the campaign chairman can come up with something better.

The best name yet devised, wherever it applies, is Building for Youth Campaign. This can be appropriate whether the project is a new church building, a new educational plant, or modernization of an old structure.

Whatever the name, it should be featured in letters to the membership, in sermons, in three-minute addresses to the congregation at worship and in Sunday-school classes, in the campaign brochure, and in news stories and all other media of promotion and publicity. By the end of the canvass the campaign name should be as familiar as that of the church itself.

An apt slogan, if one can be found, will add to the effectiveness of the effort. Here's a suggestion: "Give as Christians so that our children may live as Christians." This may start some original thinking on the subject.

A basic appeal—a primary reason why the building is needed that will touch the emotions of the prospective contributors—should be carefully chosen and then emphasized in all publicity. All other good reasons for the project should be explored and lined up for the workers, who will find that some individuals are more influenced by these other appeals. But too wide a variety of appeals in the publicity and general promotion might confuse the members. It is more effective to concentrate on one basic appeal and bring in other reasons in a supplementary way.

Whenever it applies, the most powerful basic appeal is the need of children and youth. It will move the adults of the church whether they have children of their own or not. Therefore the promotion for any project that involves educational quarters should constantly emphasize the inadequacy of the present facilities for Christian training of the boys and girls, and the improvements the new building will make possible for them. Their religious, social, and recreational needs must be dramatized over and over again. New ideas should be found for attracting attention, but they should all keep pounding on the same theme—the needs of our young people. Repetition is an essential element in good advertising, and the church will do well to use a technique which has been found effective in the commercial world.

The youth appeal of course will not be appropriate for every campaign. In a mortgage-lifting effort, for instance, the emphasis will be on freeing the church from the burden of debt and the constant drain of interest payments. A date for "burning the mortgage" may be set and the program planned, with the pastor or board chairman officiating.

In a campaign to purchase a new church site interest will center on the building to be erected later, and the basic appeal may well be to the desire of the members for a beautiful place of worship and Christian fellowship. The promotion will include much use of architect's sketches, interior floor plans, and any other available means for helping the members visualize the future building. In such a case the primary emphasis may be on the church as a whole, but much attention should be given to the needs of the children and youth.

In some other campaign for a new church site the plans for the building may not be so far along, and a better basic appeal may be the need of the community for a church. Survey data about the population of the neighborhood, the prospects for its growth, the distance to other churches, and the like can be used to good advantage. However, cold statistics must be brought to life in terms of people, and dramatizing the need in terms of children and youth will make the strongest impression.

Memorial gifts are frequently promoted in connection with building projects. This is a risky business unless early planning is done. If handled right it's a good technique to secure large pledges from certain of the members who would otherwise give only an average amount. If not, it may lead to difficulties; and some churches have avoided the plan on this account.

Here are a few precautions that may save later resentment from some who feel that their offers of help are not appreciated:

1. As soon as a decision to proceed with a building operation has been made, announce that a Memorial Gifts Commit-

tee is to be appointed to make up a list of suggested memorials to be submitted to the members. Request tactfully that nothing be done until the committee has made its report.

2. The committee should list only expensive items. Begin with five hundred, or even a thousand dollars, depending on the giving capacity of the members who have been selected as likely prospects.

3. List only those things which are needed immediately. In other words, these are articles that must be purchased out of the general building-fund proceeds unless they are financed as memorials. A rose window, for instance, is not indispensable and may be postponed till the building itself is secure.

4. Let it be known that publicity will be given to donors and to those who are to be remembered, unless otherwise requested, but that names will not be placed on memorials. This custom, once widely used, carries the wrong emphasis and is out of date.

5. Invest full power in the Memorial Committee members and back them up in any decision they may make.

6. Announce that all memorial gifts will of course apply on the campaign objective.

Wisely used, the memorial-gift plan may produce a substantial amount in added money.

A *unit-cost plan* is frequently used to intensify the appeal by centering attention on a particular fraction or unit of the total cost. One church financed the purchase of a building lot by "selling" frontage at thirty dollars a foot. A number of the children, at the suggestion of their parents, had a good lesson in stewardship by subscribing for an inch or two of the total, to be paid for out of their allowances. A diagram of the property was drawn on a large board, with the sections blacked out as they were sold.

Another church "sold" seats in the new sanctuary, with the total cost of the structure divided by the number of people who could be accommodated in the pews. In this way the over-all figures were broken down into manageable units. It proved to be an effective device.

Other units might be the number of square feet, cubic feet, bricks, or cement blocks in the building. Anything that will vizualize the size and proportions of the undertaking will be of value.

Personnel

The first essential in any finance campaign is a good leader for the drive. The *campaign chairman* is the most important figure in the undertaking. The man chosen to assume this position of leadership should be spiritual-minded, with a genuine understanding of the mission of the church, and at the same time popular with the congregation in the best sense of the word. A natural leader, he must be able to promote an enthusiastic following on the part of the entire membership. As general manager of the whole enterprise he must have some knowledge of organizational methods and be recognized for his ability to get things done.

There may be a tendency to appoint some person to the job who is prominent in the business or professional world because his position will carry weight in the community. This will be a mistake if the individual feels that all he can give is the use of his name. If the name on the letterhead will have value, such a person can be made honorary chairman and his support of the movement can be given publicity. But the man needed for the actual working leadership is the steady, dependable, month-by-month and year-by-year servant of the church whose record as a loyal member and lay leader has gained for him the affectionate respect of the congregation. The effort will have its best chance for success under his leadership.

There should be a small Campaign Committee to advise with the chairman. This group may include the chairman, the pastor, the advance-gifts chairman, and one or two other leaders who can meet frequently before and during the canvass. This committee shares with the chairman the responsibility for planning the campaign and supervising its progress, especially as regards selecting other personnel and making sure that all are performing their tasks at the right time. It should meet often throughout the campaign—and particularly during the week of solicitation—to evaluate results, strengthen weak spots in the organization, devise new strategy when necessary, and finally plan and promote adequate follow-up to the campaign.

The pastor is a key figure in the campaign. This is stated advisedly and with emphasis. Some church leaders may feel that the pastor should be left free to carry on his spiritual ministry while the laymen take over the job of raising the money. This may show a praiseworthy sense of responsibility, but, as has been emphasized already, the spiritual elements are the foundation for any church fund-raising campaign. Though stressing the religious side of the effort must not be left to the pastor alone, it will depend largely on him. He can probably see more clearly, and express more effectively, the ultimate goals toward which the whole effort is aimed. Specifically through stewardship sermons and through planning and promoting prayer groups he can lead the congregation to see their undertaking in a divine light.

Furthermore the pastor is likely to know the personnel of the church and their capacities as no one else can. His guidance in choosing committee members and other workers is generally indispensable.

The fact is that the conscientious pastor will be a bit resentful if he is left on the side lines while the game is on, even on the plea that he should not be bothered with the financial affairs of the church. As the leader of his people, he will wish to serve their best interests in any and every capacity. He shouldn't be robbed of a chance to feel the joy and pride of an active participant when the drive goes over and the victory is won.

The office secretary is a most important cog in the campaign machinery. A smoothly running organization, with things done on time and ready when needed, will be due to the secretary more than anyone else. Good work in this department will save the campaign chairman many a headache.

If there's a regular church secretary, well and good. If not, the chairman should hire someone. Do not depend on volunteer help. Open an office in the church building or other convenient location, install a desk, chair, and telephone, and maintain a regular schedule of office hours during the period of preparation and the duration of the campaign.

Ideally the secretary should be someone who has been in the church office a number of years. At least she should know everybody and be aware of what is going on in every department of the church life. She can help the campaign chairman with her suggestions and assist the division generals and captains in securing fill-ins on incomplete teams. It goes without saying that she must be friendly and co-operative—in short, a good public-relations person for the church.

She must follow through carefully on the items described in the chapter on preparing materials—make out the prospect list and type in the names of member families on the cards for the campaign and office files. Her work will include addressing envelopes and mailing the two general letters, preparing the worker's kits and getting the cards ready for distribution at the Workers' Dinner. Later of course she will have much to do with handling the pledges as they come in and supplying reports of progress and of prospects still to be visited.

Special committees to handle various tasks in connection with the campaign are quite desirable. The more jobs that can be handed around, the better. The chairman will hatch up everything he can think of and delegate responsibility for it to a committee. The members will attend meetings, discuss problems, and become more interested in their church. They will also give more when the time for signing pledges comes around. Here are a few suggestions:

1. Campaign Committee—as previously mentioned, to have general charge, under the leadership of the chairman, from the first day until the last.

2. Advance Gifts Committee—to solicit members from whom the bigger gifts should be received.

3. Evaluations Committee—to estimate a "goal" for each prospect, taking into account the total campaign goal and the giving capacity of the prospect. Total evaluations should equal about twice the campaign goal.

4. Dinner Committee—to have charge of the various dinner events. A different group of women may be appointed for each event to spread the work around.

5. Decorating Committee—to see that the dining room and tables are decorated with flowers, fluted crepe strips of different colors, flags, bunting, posters, and any other means of giving the place a festive appearance.

6. Audit Committee—to check on pledges as they are received and see that accurate amounts are recorded. In the small campaign this work can be handled by the office secretary or church treasurer. Otherwise it should be taken over by one or two people who are experienced in office detail. Checking of all reports should be done not later than the next morning after they are handed in.

7. Children's Committee—to care for small children when their parents are attending any of the dinner events. A room should be set aside, with an experienced children's worker in attendance. A special table may be set up in the dining room for the children's meals. Using a lettered sign, "The Church of Tomorrow," will have an added appeal. After the meal the children go to their own room for games or movies.

8. Telephone Committee—a group of women who will telephone workers and urge attendance at the various campaign events.

9. Publicity Committee—to see that every possible method is used in keeping the congregation informed and interested, and in planning and providing campaign publicity materials.

10. Training Committee—to teach workers how to solicit pledges. This will usually center in one man who has had selling experience or taught salesmanship. It may be the campaign chairman or anyone else who has special qualifications. There will be many in the working organization who have never done anything like this before. They will need help.

The soliciting personnel will of course include many who are also serving on some of the committees. The number of member families in the congregation will determine the size of the working organization, which should be large enough so that only about five cards need be assigned to each worker. The usual practice is to have about six workers form a team and from three to five teams make up a division, each team being headed by a captain and each division by a general. The workers solicit all the member families except those seen by the advance-gifts group.

The time schedule

Time is an important factor in a campaign—as regards both the best date and the schedule of events within the period selected.

What is the best season of the year to hold the campaign? Certainly the hot months in the southern and temperate zones must be ruled out. And in the north, winter cold and storms would cut down attendance at meetings and reduce the enthusiasm of the workers. The geographical location of the church is therefore a factor in the choice. Generally speaking, the fall and spring months are to be favored, though successful campaigns have been held in all seasons of the year when emergencies made immediate action imperative—a church fire, for instance, of which there are altogether too many.

If the annual canvass for the church budget is held in the fall, the natural choice of a date for the building campaign would be sometime during the spring, and vice versa. Occasionally these two canvasses are conducted in one operation, using two pledge cards. But this is to be avoided if possible. It's better to shoot at a single objective.

The pre-Christmas and pre-Easter seasons are also to be avoided. In December it is hard to divert the attention of the members from the coming Christmas festivities, even if a "gift for the church" emphasis is used. In the period just before Easter many churches now put on a personal-visitation evangelism campaign—an effective plan for securing new members that should not be interrupted or omitted. In the main therefore, unless there are obstacles in the way, the best periods for campaigning are the months of September, October, and November in the fall and the season in the spring beginning about two weeks after Easter and extending into early summer.

The opinion is held by some people that the federal-tax-payment period in mid-March is an unfavorable time for a campaign, but it is to be doubted whether this has any marked bearing on the results of a properly conducted canvass.

To keep up with the details of the campaign after the date has been set, the chairman is advised to prepare a calendar of events and processes very early in the planning period. This is done so that each part of the operation may fall into its proper place. When active solicitation begins, everything to the last detail must be ready. If full preparations are not made, confusion and delay will be experienced.

A suggested calendar for a campaign is shown on the following pages, with the items distributed among three weeks of preparation and one week of solicitation. For actual use the Campaign Committee should date the items on its calendar by days rather than simply weeks. In some cases the committee may find it wise to include another week in the preparatory period, and it should be prepared to decide on a last-minute extension of the solicitation for an extra week in case the job is not completed in one week.

As outlined here, the first public event of the campaign is a Loyalty Dinner, to which every member of the church is invited, to receive information about the building project and the campaign. This is followed up immediately by a letter from the campaign chairman to each member family, enclosing an attractive printed brochure containing pictures and information to reinforce what was said at the dinner. At this time the Advance Gifts Committee begins special solicitation of selected persons expected to make large pledges. Meanwhile various types of publicity continue, posters are prepared, and a large thermometer or other device to show the progress of the campaign is displayed in a prominent place. The teams of workers are completed, and the names of captains and generals are painted on a large scoreboard beside spaces which will later be filled in at the report meetings as the amounts for each team are announced. During the week before the solicitation the pastor sends out a letter to each member. Toward the end of the week there is a Workers' Dinner, at which the solicitors receive their assignments, materials, and instructions. The following Sunday they meet again for luncheon after the morning service and then immediately go out to start soliciting. The solicitation continues throughout this week—or longer if necessary—and frequent report meetings are scheduled.

FIRST WEEK

Campaign Chairman
  Plan program for Loyalty Dinner
  Get pledge cards printed
  Order envelopes for weekly or monthly payments on pledges
  Appoint division generals
  Prepare list of prospective team captains
  Call meeting of generals to choose team captains

Pastor
  Assist in plans for Loyalty Dinner
  Assist in preparing list of prospective team captains

Office Secretary
  Check prospect list carefully
  Send out invitations for Loyalty Dinner
  Copy names of prospects on pledge cards (campaign file)
  Copy names on blank cards (office file)
  Mimeograph captains' report envelopes and workers' envelopes

Dinner Committee
  Plan food and service for Loyalty Dinner

Evaluations Committee
  Make evaluations and note on backs of prospect cards

Publicity Committee
  Prepare letterhead and envelope to match
  Prepare brochure
  Prepare audio-visual promotional materials

SECOND WEEK

Campaign Chairman

Preside over Loyalty Dinner early in week

Assist in withdrawing advance-gifts cards from campaign file

Write letter of thanks to team captains

Prepare list of prospective workers

Assist in preparing letter to congregation

Call meeting of team captains to choose workers

Pastor

Get prayer-league cards signed

Assist in holding Loyalty Dinner

Assist in withdrawing advance-gifts cards from campaign file

Assist in preparing list of prospective workers

Office Secretary

Mail campaign chairman's letter to congregation as soon as brochure is received from printer

Mail campaign chairman's letter of thanks to team captains

Make up assignments of prospects to teams

Mimeograph list of prospective workers

Mimeograph card receipts

Publicity Committee

Make announcements in all church meetings Sunday and during the week

Present audio-visual materials in meetings where time permits

Prepare letter from campaign chairman to congregation (enclose brochure)

Assist in writing letter of thanks to team captains from campaign chairman

Get copy for thermometer in hands of commercial artist

Work on place cards and poster or slogan contest

Advance Gifts Committee

Withdraw advance-gifts cards from campaign file

Begin canvass as soon as letter and brochure reach congregation

Division Generals

Sign up all team captains early in week.

Decorating Committee

Decorate dining room for Loyalty Dinner

Dinner Committee

Cook and serve food at Loyalty Dinner

Plan food and service for Workers' Dinner

THIRD WEEK

Campaign Chairman

Write letter of thanks to signed-up workers, urging attendance at Workers' Dinner

Check work of all committees to see that everything is ready

Preside over Workers' Dinner on Thursday or Friday night

Pastor

Hold sectional prayer meetings or prayer programs

Write letter to members to be ready to mail by Thursday or before (enclose stewardship leaflet if desired)

In morning service stress attendance at Workers' Dinner

Assist in holding Workers' Dinner on Thursday or Friday night

Office Secretary

Mail letters of thanks to signed-up workers as names come in

Mail letter from pastor to members

Provide team assignments, workers' kits, and other supplies at Workers' Dinner

Morning after Workers' Dinner enter information from card receipts in office file

Publicity Committee

Make announcements in all church meetings

Present audio-visual materials in meetings where time permits

Prepare scoreboard as soon as names of team captains are known

Finish thermometer and set up in dining room

Prepare stories and pictures for Sunday paper

Prepare radio and television announcements

Assist in getting letter to members from pastor ready to mail by Thursday

Division Generals

Check on progress of team captains in signing up workers

Telephone Committee

Call all workers day before Workers' Dinner

Decorating Committee

Decorate dining room for Workers' Dinner

Dinner Committee

Cook and serve food at Workers' Dinner on Thursday or Friday night

Plan food and service for Campaign Sunday Luncheon

Training Committee

Make plans for training workers at Workers' Dinner (or at special session)

CAMPAIGN WEEK

Campaign Chairman

Make strong appeal in Sunday morning service

Preside over Campaign Sunday Luncheon

Conduct report meetings at eight o'clock Sunday, Wednesday, Friday (or Tuesday, Thursday), and Sunday nights

Make analysis of pledges

Initiate emergency measures if trend is unfavorable

Extend campaign one week if necessary and hold such additional report meetings as are needed

Pastor

Deliver appropriate sermon Sunday morning

Encourage workers at report meetings

Office Secretary

Collect pledges and reports from team captains at report meetings

Audit returns, if Audit Committee was not appointed

Keep office file up to date as reports are received

Assist in making analysis of pledges

Mail page of team standings to team workers late in week

Mail list of unworked cards to reach each team captain and campaign chairman by Saturday

Audit Committee (optional)

Audit returns

Dinner Committee

Cook and serve food at Campaign Sunday Luncheon

Workers

Carry on solicitation from one to four o'clock Sunday and six to eight o'clock daily

Preparing Materials 3

While the planning process described in the previous chapter is still going on, work must begin on the materials to be used.

The first job for the office secretary is a careful checking of the membership roll of the church. This must be done very early—before other things begin to crowd in. Some pastors and office secretaries are careful to keep their records up to date. Others are lax. In either case the first step is to scrutinize every name and address on the roll. If there is doubt, inquiry should be made so that the record is correct in every detail. Telephone books and city directories should be used for checking addresses. Team workers who give time and effort to the solicitation deserve to have correct names and addresses on the cards which are handed to them. It is highly irritating to be told that "Mr. Smith moved away from here three years ago," or "Mr. Jones died a year ago last June."

Up-to-the-minute records in large churches are hard to maintain. Changes in addresses are made often, and rare is the person who calls the church office to register the new street and number. Yet the harried pastor, by some occult means, is supposed to know the new address and make his appearance there in due time, though he has no knowledge whatever of what has become of this "lost" family. It is well to explain this problem to the team workers when the canvass begins. They should know why some of the information on their cards may be faulty. Further, their aid should be asked in following through on removals and address changes and reporting back to the church office.

While the greater part of the money will come from the church members, there are other sources of income that should not be neglected. There are public-spirited citizens, not members of any church, in every town and city who will give to a church-building campaign. Careful selection of the people to call on them must be made. Another source might be two or three business or industrial concerns which are represented in the membership. An employee, preferably one of executive standing, should make the appeal. These names should be added to the membership roll to form the prospect list.

Prospect cards

While the process of checking names and addresses and making up the full prospect list is going on, the pledge cards may be printed so as to be ready for use in assigning the prospects to the solicitors. Good-quality, stiff paper stock should be used; and three times as many as there are families in the membership will be needed. Figures 1 and 2 show the arrangement and wording of typical pledge cards for weekly and monthly payments. The over-all size is four by eight inches, and when the receipt stubs are removed, the cards fit a six-inch file. A card of this size is better than a smaller one because it provides more room for copy.

With the names on the prospect list in alphabetical order, the office secretary will type the names of the first family— for instance, Mr. and Mrs. John Adams—and their address

Figure 1

Pledge Card for Weekly Payments

In consideration of the gifts of others, I will endeavor to pay *each week* the sum of $_____ to the (name of campaign and church) for the erection of a modern educational building for the Christian training of the boys and girls of the membership and community.

The payments will be continued for 52 weeks, beginning with Sunday (include date).

Total Pledge $_____ Cash $_____

As an alternative, I will pay as follows:

Signed_____ Address_____

Solicitor_____ Team Number_____

No_____

Date_____

Received, with thanks, from _____ in cash to apply on pledge to the sum of $ _____ the (name of campaign).

Signed_____

Date_____

Figure 2

Pledge Card for Monthly Payments

In consideration of the gifts of others, I will subscribe the sum of $_____ to be paid each month to the Church Enlargement Fund of Olivet Presbyterian Church for the erection of a modern, well-equipped building for the Christian training of the boys and girls and young people of the membership and community and for many other purposes in the church program.

The monthly payments will continue for 36 months, beginning with May, 1953. Total Pledge $_____ Cash $_____.

As an alternative to the above plan, I will pay as follows:

Signed_____ Address_____

Solicitor_____ Team Number_____

No_____

Date_____

Received from _____ with deep appreciation the sum of $ _____ for the Church Enlargement Fund of the Olivet Presbyterian Church.

Signed_____

Date_____

in the top margin of a pledge card. She will add the names of any employed persons in the family and any relatives living with them who are members of the church. This card should be numbered 1 in the upper right corner. The next family goes on the second card, numbered 2, and so on through the list. For later insertions, after the list is completed, use letters—16a, 16b, and so on. There should be few of these in the carefully checked prospect list.

Typing the names on the pledge cards turns them into prospect cards, and the whole group of them forms what may be called the "campaign file." These are the cards which the workers will use in making their calls.

Before beginning the next step, the secretary should check these cards for duplications. Letters will be addressed to these names later, and any family receiving more than one may charge the church with "wasting money."

Next make a duplicate of the campaign file, using blank cards of different size or different color, to prevent confusion. Type the names and addresses exactly as on the other cards and put the same numbers in the upper right corners. When this is done, check carefully to see that Mr. and Mrs. William Smith have the same number on both of their cards in the two files. If there are any mistakes, it will cause trouble later. This set of cards may be known as the "office file" and should be kept for the sole use of the pastor, campaign chairman, and secretary. On these cards will be entered later the names of the workers who have agreed to see these prospects and also the results of the calls after the interviews are over.

The numbering system facilitates a thorough follow-through on card assignments. Far too many campaigns have failed because the prospects were not seen, the "cards were not worked." Team workers start out on their calls with the best intentions in the world, but unless they are spurred on from time to time, some of them will fall by the wayside. This problem, present in every canvass without exception, will be mentioned several times in these pages; and a workable plan will be outlined which will assure practically complete coverage.

Card evaluations

Evaluation is a device by which the member may learn what it is "hoped" he will pledge. He may not give that much, or he may give more, but it is a definite figure for his consideration. Used tactfully, the plan will increase the average giving materially. This operation used to be known as "rating" the cards, but the word has unfortunate implications: "evaluating" is a better term. It is done by families rather than by individuals. If there are single employed persons or in-laws in the family circle, they may be evaluated also.

The Evaluations Committee should be made up of individuals who know the financial standing and giving capacity of a large number of the members. They will likely be bank officers and credit-association people. Lacking these, certain of the well-known board members will be the next best choice.

The evaluation total must of course be fitted to the amount to be raised. Let's take a $50,000 goal. The committee makes a test run-through of the members, estimating what each can give. The total should reach about $100,000—twice the goal. This doubling is necessary because many will not give what is expected and some will not give at all. If the total falls short of $100,000, the figures must be revised upward until the desired amount is reached. Of course if several large gifts are in prospect, the evaluation may differ slightly all along the line.

The next step is to indicate the evaluation on each card. Some have had the cards made up with an extra perforated stub, in addition to the receipt, on which to write the evaluations. This is torn off before the worker calls on the prospect. A simpler method is to pencil the amount on the back of the card, where the prospect is not likely to see it.

If the weekly payment plan is used, the evaluation should be in the same terms—$50, $25, $10, $5, and so on. For simpler calculation the year is usually considered to run for fifty weeks, and a little multiplication is needed to get the total for comparison with the goal.

If the monthly payment plan is employed, the evaluations should be in terms of $150, $100, $50, and so on, per month, to be multiplied by twelve, twenty-four, or thirty-six.

Informing the members that evaluations have been made is a delicate matter. Some easily take offense if they think that someone else is presuming to tell them what they should give. At the best, certain folks will have their feelings hurt when they learn their evaluations. But it is a risk that must be taken. The more dependable members who habitually give the most money will almost always take it in good part.

Brief mention might be made of the plan in one of the letters which will be sent out to all member families. Some experienced campaign directors insist that the member should be informed that no mention of his evaluation will be made unless he asks for it. Many of them will ask out of curiosity. Others feel that the worker should be free to mention the amount, in case the prospect doesn't ask, if a good opportunity is presented.

The best places to explain the plan will be at the Loyalty Dinner, at one of the morning services, and at meetings of the workers. This will include around 75 per cent of the members. An appeal for understanding might be something like the following:

"We need fifty thousand dollars in weekly payment pledges. If our canvass is to succeed, we must have enough in cash and pledges to reach this figure. How can we do this? Our best chance is to profit by the experience of others. They have been successful with what is known as the 'evaluation plan.' If we use this method, our chances are good; if we don't, they are poor.

"The plan is worked through a committee. In our case this group, with our fifty-thousand-dollar goal in mind, has been asked to estimate what each member family might give in order to reach the amount needed. No attempt is made to tell the member what he *should* give nor what he is *expected* to give nor what he is '*down for*.' No one knows what another should give in this canvass; that is a matter between him and his God. All we are asking is that the member consider the evaluated amount for him and then give as his conscience may direct.

"We are hoping that the general membership will accept the plan in good spirit. We all want to succeed. This is the way it can be done. Other churches have used it and found it good. It worked for them. It will work for us."

The committee will be puzzled to know how to evaluate the people they don't know—the seldom-attenders and the non-givers. The only thing to do is to give them a high minimum and let it go at that. This would be about one dollar on the weekly basis and five dollars on the monthly.

Materials for Solicitors

Work on the prospect list should begin as soon as a decision to carry on the canvass is made. This should be followed at once by the printing of the pledge cards and the making of the campaign and office files, and then by the preparation of other materials that will be needed.

Certain mimeographed items can be run off very early, so as to save time later. When the canvass starts, it moves at high speed; and any lack of materials when they are needed will prove to be costly.

Card receipts are used by the workers to set down the numbers on the prospect cards which they choose. This information is then transferred to the office file, and the worker's task is not finished until he has made a report on every card he has agreed to work. Getting this record is part of the plan to secure complete coverage on all prospects. About one fifth as many receipts as there are families will be needed. They can be run off on mimeograph paper by filling a stencil with the forms and separating with a paper cutter. Any small size will do. Suggested wording appears in Figure 3.

I have taken the cards numbered below, and
will see these prospects as soon as I can.

Numbers:

Signed ....

Team No. ....

Figure 3
Card Receipt

Workers' envelopes are needed to hold the materials supplied to the workers and to provide them with a convenient means for carrying their prospect cards. Use size 11 or 12 envelopes, enough to give each worker one, and mimeograph on the face something like the following:

INSTRUCTIONS FOR TEAM WORKERS

Choose five or six cards at your team meeting.
Fill out receipt for cards you pick and hand to your captain.

Make your own pledge before seeing others.

See all prospects early. DO IT NOW!

Call-backs may be necessary. Follow through till you get your man.

Report changes of address on cards.

If no address can be found, note on card and turn back to your captain.

Hand all completed cards to your captain at each report meeting, as follows:

(List schedule of report meetings.)

Work every card and do it soon.

A great challenge faces our church. Devotion to the cause, prayer, generous giving, and hard work will bring victory.

CAPTAIN'S REPORT ENVELOPE			
Captain			
Team No. .... Date			
Prospect No.	Number of Pledges	Total Pledged	Cash
Totals			
Number cards assigned			
Number worked			
Number yet to work			

Figure 4
Captain's Report Envelope

A day or two before the Workers' Dinner place in each envelope a copy of the printed brochure (with any other promotional materials to supply the workers with ammunition), a card receipt, five extra blank pledge cards, and a half-dozen paper clips and rubber bands. On the night of the dinner one of these kits is put at each place.

Report envelopes provide an efficient way for the workers to make reports and turn in the cards they have completed. Figure 4 shows suggested copy. They should be the same size as the workers' envelopes, but a different color helps to prevent confusion. Make five times as many as there are teams. If the number of teams is not known at this time, make one fifth as many as the number of families to be canvassed. In big campaigns report envelopes may be prepared for individual team workers. In the average canvass envelopes for the captains will be enough. Each team will then report in one envelope at each report meeting.

Place cards, large enough to read across the room, are needed for the Workers' Dinner and the Campaign Sunday Luncheon in order to get the teams together. They should be well-lettered, stiff cards, done in several colors, which will stand alone. Window-card stock of full-sheet size will cut up into 11- by 14-inch pieces. These are a good size for the top leaders and can be cut in two for the team markers. Include the campaign chairman, chairman of advance gifts, pastor, and division generals on the big cards. Put the captain's name on each team card. If the cocaptain plan is used, put on both names. Letter the title as well as the name—for instance, "Division A—General George Washington," "Team 1—Captains Mr. and Mrs. John Alden." Supports for the cards can be made by cutting a 2x4 board into 4-inch lengths and then sawing a crosswise slit to the depth of a half- or three-quarter inch.

A thermometer, or similar large graph, for visualizing the progress of the canvass is always good for keeping up the enthusiasm of the workers. It may be placed in the church for a week or two before the canvass opens, if there are no objections. After that it would be used at the dinner events and all report meetings, with the center painted up in red to the proper level after the reports are made. The campaign chairman's wife, the advance-gifts chairman's wife, and a young child or two should be invited to do the painting. A one-inch brush and small can of red paint are required.

Figure 5 is based on the thermometer used in a campaign that raised more than 10 per cent above its goal. The over-all

Figure 5
Thermometer

height was about seven or eight feet, with stilts two feet high. It was framed so as to stand against the wall.

A scoreboard on which the reports from each team can be entered and totaled at each report meeting is very valuable for keeping up the spirit of the workers. It permits the use of many names, which always builds up the sense of personal responsibility. It also gives the campaign chairman a way to emphasize that he expects a report from every captain at every report meeting—there must be no vacant spaces on the board. Nothing dampens the spirits of a working group more than "no report" from several of the teams. A well-filled scoreboard encourages good work; workers like to make good reports and see the amounts go up on the wall.

A series of Sunday-school blackboards will answer the purpose, but it is well worth the time and money to provide something more attractive and substantial. The actual scoreboard which supplied the names and amounts of Figure 6 was constructed from a 4- by 8-foot piece of masonite with the lines, headings, and names painted on over an all-over coating that would take white chalk. The reports of advance gifts and later of the campaign total were entered on another board at one side, but in other cases might be on the same board. In this example only two vacant spaces show up, and one of these occurred because the team had finished its cards.

DIVISION "A" Gen. Geo. Goerlitz

REPORTS	Oct.5	Oct.8	Total	Oct.10	Total	Oct.12	TEAM TOTAL
TEAM NO.1 CAPTS. ROBINSON	1616 ⁰⁰	375 ⁰⁰	1991 ⁰⁰	435 ⁰⁰	2426 ⁰⁰	485 ⁰⁰	2911 ⁰⁰
TEAM NO.2 CAPTS. KOUTS	1482 ⁰⁰	200 ⁰⁰	1682 ⁰⁰	150 ⁰⁰	1832 ⁰⁰	510 ⁰⁰	2342 ⁰⁰
TEAM NO.3 CAPTS. BERRYMAN	550 ⁰⁰	450 ⁰⁰	1000 ⁰⁰	650 ⁰⁰	1650 ⁰⁰	150 ⁰⁰	1800 ⁰⁰
DIVISION TOTAL	3648 ⁰⁰	1025 ⁰⁰	4673 ⁰⁰	1235 ⁰⁰	5908 ⁰⁰	1145 ⁰⁰	7053 ⁰⁰

DIVISION "C" Gen. Don. Judd

REPORTS	Oct.5	Oct.8	Total	Oct.10	Total	Oct.12	TEAM TOTAL
TEAM NO.7 CAPTS. DETRAZ	315 ⁰⁰	722 ⁰⁰	1037 ⁰⁰	410 ⁰⁰	1447 ⁰⁰	600 ⁰⁰	2047 ⁰⁰
TEAM NO.8 CAPTS. FUQUAY	2375 ⁰⁰	350 ⁰⁰	2725 ⁰⁰	875 ⁰⁰	3600 ⁰⁰	30 ⁰⁰	3630 ⁰⁰
TEAM NO.9 CAPTS. SCHROEDER & CRISP	835 ⁰⁰	632 ⁰⁰	1467 ⁰⁰	1045 ⁰⁰	2512 ⁰⁰	360 ⁰⁰	2872 ⁰⁰
DIVISION TOTAL	3525 ⁰⁰	1704 ⁰⁰	5229 ⁰⁰	2330 ⁰⁰	7559 ⁰⁰	990 ⁰⁰	8549 ⁰⁰

DIVISION "B" Gen. Rvie Hartig

REPORTS	Oct.5	Oct.8	Total	Oct.10	Total	Oct.12	TEAM TOTAL
TEAM NO.4 CAPTS. BROTHER	1695 ⁰⁰	180 ⁰⁰	1875 ⁰⁰	100 ⁰⁰	1975 ⁰⁰		1975 ⁰⁰
TEAM NO.5 CAPTS. EDWARDS	1815 ⁰⁰	1556 ²⁰	3371 ²⁰	150 ⁰⁰	3521 ²⁰	825 ⁰⁰	4346 ²⁰
TEAM NO.6 CAPTS. STOVALL	1020 ⁰⁰	895 ⁰⁰	1915 ⁰⁰	735 ⁰⁰	2650 ⁰⁰	258 ⁰⁰	2908 ⁰⁰
DIVISION TOTAL	4530 ⁰⁰	2631 ²⁰	7161 ²⁰	985 ⁰⁰	8146 ²⁰	1083 ⁰⁰	9221 ²⁰

DIVISION "D" Gen. Mel. Smart

REPORTS	Oct.5	Oct.8	Total	Oct.10	Total	Oct.12	TEAM TOTAL
TEAM NO.10 CAPTS. HEADLEE & SANDLEBEN	2200 ⁰⁰	2086 ⁰⁰	4286 ⁰⁰	50 ⁰⁰	4336 ⁰⁰	200 ⁰⁰	4536 ⁰⁰
TEAM NO.11 CAPTS. GEARING	2100 ⁰⁰	32 ⁰⁰	2132 ⁰⁰	2350 ⁰⁰	4482 ⁰⁰	430 ⁰⁰	4912 ⁰⁰
TEAM NO.12 CAPTS. DRICKEY	946 ⁰⁰	320 ⁰⁰	1266 ⁰⁰		1266 ⁰⁰	702 ⁰⁰	1968 ⁰⁰
DIVISION TOTAL	5246 ⁰⁰	2438 ⁰⁰	7684 ⁰⁰	2400 ⁰⁰	10840 ⁰⁰	1332 ²²	11416 ⁰⁰

Figure 6
Scoreboard

A scoreboard with but one actual vacancy shows a high degree of loyal service.

Envelopes for payments on pledges should be ready by the time of the Workers' Dinner. Therefore they must be ordered very early—just as soon as a decision is made on the length of the period over which payments will run and whether payments are to be made on a weekly or monthly basis. These facts must be known in order to get the right number. For instance, if payments are to run for one year on the weekly payment basis, fifty-two envelopes will be needed for each contributor. If for three years on the monthly payment plan, thirty-six will be required. They should differ from the regular annual canvass envelopes, both in color and in size.

The Campaign Committee must decide on a plan for getting the envelopes into the hands of the contributors. Usually it is the same method as that employed in sending out the annual canvass cartons. Mailing is the easiest and most efficient way, and this can be done immediately after the close of the campaign so that payments can begin the following Sunday or by the first of the following month. Unless mailing has been the custom previously, the members should be informed that this plan will be used. It can be explained in some of the publicity and by announcement from the pulpit. Also the workers should be reminded of the plan at the Workers' Dinner.

Some churches send the packets right along with the canvassers. This works out very well if the workers will always remember to take the envelopes with them when they make their calls and will remember to leave them with the contributors when they come away.

Whatever the method, prompt action is needed so that the pledges will be encouraged to begin payments immediately after the canvass closes.

Promotional materials

The Publicity Committee must get off to an early start in its promotional campaign. Its members should be chosen as soon as possible and should begin their work right away. They should aim at employing every legitimate means toward a psychological and spiritual build-up of interest and loyalty among the members and must start by preparing effective materials.

A *letterhead* that is well designed and well printed adds dignity and importance to the project and is a big help in getting attention and stimulating interest. The name chosen for the campaign should be printed across the top of the page. Underneath it include the name of the church, the town or city, the campaign goal, the date of the canvass, and the names of the pastor, chairman, division generals, and committee chairmen—the more names the better. A tasteful two-color printing job will make the letterhead more attractive. An example of an actual letterhead used in a recent canvass is shown in Figure 7.

The letterhead will be used for mailings to the membership, thank-you notes and reminders to workers, and miscellaneous correspondence connected with the campaign. The most effective plan for letters to the members is to send one from the campaign chairman at the beginning of the build-up period, enclosing a printed brochure about the building project and the campaign, and a second from the pastor the week before the general canvass begins, perhaps enclosing a leaflet on tithing or some other phase of stewardship.

Envelopes to match the letterhead are needed, of course; and they must be of the right size to carry the enclosures that will go with the letters. Weight is also important, for all letters should be sent by first-class mail, and a slight

Church Enlargement Fund Campaign

OLIVET PRESBYTERIAN CHURCH
Evansville, Indiana
Pastor: Dr. J. V. Roth

Campaign Week May 3 to 10   Goal $60,000

"IT CAN BE DONE"

CAMPAIGN CHAIRMAN
Carlton B. Sexson

CHAIRMAN ADVANCE GIFTS
Blake D. Foster

CHAIRMAN PUBLICITY
Wendell Marsh

CHAIRMAN SPEAKERS COM.
Earl Smith

CHAIRMAN CHILDRENS' COM.
Mrs. George Blackburn

CHAIRMEN DINNER COM.
Mrs. Thomas Fowler
Mrs. Clyde Mauer

Dear Friends:

HERE ARE THREE QUESTIONS ONLY YOU CAN ANSWER

1 Is it possible for Olivet to finance, without one dollar of long-term debt, the beautiful new building now going up on the church lot? (It will require, of course, a temporary loan to current building costs).

2 Can Olivet neglect any longer ligation to provide a tho

Figure 7
Letterhead and Letter

fraction of excess weight might double the cost of postage. Before the printing begins, blank sheets, envelopes, and dummy enclosures should be checked at the post office. As soon as the envelopes come from the printer, they should be addressed, using the office file of prospect cards, so as to be ready for stuffing and mailing at the proper time.

Copy for the two letters should be prepared with the utmost effort at effectiveness in getting attention and arousing interest. If the campaign chairman wants to compose for himself the opening letter that goes out over his signature, he should at least let the experts on the Publicity Committee review it and suggest ways to make it do the job better.

The trouble with many letters is that they are too long and everything in them is too long. Such letters will not be read by many. Send a short letter—not over two thirds of a page. Keep the paragraphs short, the sentences short, and the words short. Use an eye-catching phrase at the start. A line of capitals and an underlined word here and there will get attention, but remember that too much of this makes a letter hard to read.

In this first letter center the message on the need that exists. This is what the campaign is for. The "building for youth" appeal will get the best response in most cases, and it should be stressed in every letter and piece of printed matter. At the end of the letter ask the reader to look over the enclosed brochure.

This first mailing must reach all church families before advance-gifts work begins, so careful planning is needed to get the letter and the brochure ready in time.

The second letter should be mailed several days or a week before Campaign Sunday, which is the opening of the general canvass. This may well be from the pastor and center on the spiritual aspects of the campaign. A leaflet bearing on these may be enclosed. Probably the pastor will wish to compose this letter himself. It will be a message from the heart, and he may need to agonize over it a bit before it's just right.

It goes without saying that both letters need a good job of mimeographing. The names of the signers may be written on the stencil with a stylus.

The brochure is a job for an experienced newspaperman or advertising man, and he should be allowed to spend what it takes to do the job right. Money for a well-printed, two-color brochure is money well spent. In no other way can so much information be placed in so many hands in so short a time, for this will go to every member family in the church. In fact, some of the infrequent attenders can be reached in no other way.

Big campaigns send out elaborate brochures, with many pictures and architects' sketches. For the smaller canvass an eight-page folder that will fit a size-12 envelope will answer the purpose. About five hundred will be needed for a three-hundred-family church.

The cover page must excite interest so that the reader will look within. It is believed that the samples shown in Figure 8 will encourage the member to turn the page.

Pictures tell the story on the inside pages. For example, instead of writing about the need, show a crowded classroom and beside it for contrast a view of a modern, well-lighted, well-furnished room. Use an architect's sketch of the new building and the floor plans, to let everyone see what the proposed structure will be like. Wherever possible work in view of confirmation classes, junior choirs in their robes, and other children's groups. Put a short descriptive phrase under each one.

This is the Lord's money, loaned to you, ... return?

Ho...

Whe...
do...
Lo...
w...

ten
QUESTIONS
Only You
CAN ANSWER!

...Avenue
...Church

Summons for
Jury Duty!

East Side
Christian Church
versus
Inadequate Parsonage

**YOU ARE ON THE JURY!!!
HOW DO YOU VOTE???**

Figure 8
Brochures Used
in Campaigns

If there are plenty of well-chosen pictures, only a brief announcement of the purpose, goal, and date of the campaign will be needed, with an urgent appeal for sacrificial giving.

A useful feature of the folder may be a "standard of giving" table, which should be carefully worked out. With a $50,000 goal, the following pledges, or their equivalent, are required for success, using the weekly payment plan for 150 weeks:

1 pledge for $35
1 pledge for $25
2 pledges for $15
5 pledges for $10
10 pledges for $ 5
25 pledges for $ 2
100 pledges for $ 1

The end results of the canvass will be nothing like this, of course. It is simply an attempt to picture what is required if the goal is to be reached. With larger or smaller goals the schedule will vary accordingly.

Be sure to include the names of all top leaders who have been appointed at the time the folder goes to press. This list usually appears on the last page.

A copy of this brochure in the hands of each worker will be of great value in approaching prospects:

1. It can be used to steer the interview quickly to church matters.

2. It will help in answering questions about the improvement program.

3. The "standard of giving" schedule will encourage consideration of a specific amount: "Will you be one of five to give ten dollars a week?"

Audio-visual materials offer a great promotional opportunity. The church should make good use of all the equipment it owns or can borrow.

Make colored slides or, better still, movies of crowds jamming the present inadequate facilities. Catch teachers and other leaders trying to carry out their part of the church's program against the handicaps of poor equipment. Then for contrast secure from other churches pictures of the best in modern rooms and furniture.

If the project is a new church, make pictures that will dramatize the need for a church in the neighborhood. For example, show the nearest church and then a few scenes of the traffic conditions that keep most people from going the distance to it. Take some pictures around the neighborhood that will suggest the large unchurched population and the likelihood of increasing numbers. Get some shots of young people loafing around the corner drugstore on Sunday morning when they should be in Sunday school. Especially be sure to get some appealing pictures of the smaller boys and girls of the neighborhood.

If building operations have already started, take a series of color movies of all that is going on—steam shovels excavating, trucks bringing materials, mixers pouring cement, workmen erecting the walls, and so on. If not, get pictures of the site from various angles and with various leaders of the church examining it.

In any case don't forget the people—long shots, middle shots, and close-ups. Snap them in committee meetings, board meetings, Sunday-school classes—any and every occasion where people are gathered. They'll love to see themselves on the screen.

Don't overlook the possibilities of a tape recorder also—either along with pictures or independently. Recording brief interviews with members of the church and with well-known figures of the community and of the denomination will give many an opportunity to express public endorsement of the campaign. If a well-known local radio announcer can be secured for the interviewing, lively conversations will be assured. People will listen attentively—especially those who have been interviewed.

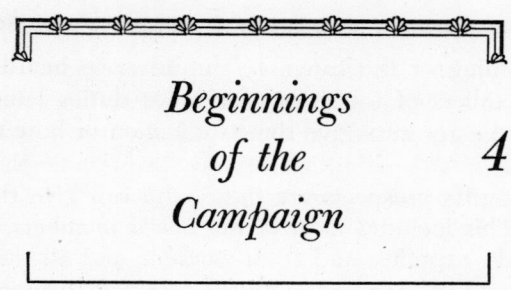

Beginnings of the Campaign

4

*N*ow *that* nearly all the plans and preparations have been made, we are ready to enter the build-up period. As far as the general membership is concerned, some big event is needed very early in this period to start the members talking, thinking, and praying about the campaign. The Loyalty Dinner, described later in this chapter, is designed for this purpose. Meanwhile some quiet work must be going on behind the scenes which is vital in reaching the campaign goal.

Advance gifts

The backbone of any finance campaign is found in its big gifts. Unless these can be had in volume, the goal cannot be reached. The importance of the work of the Advance Gifts Committee cannot be stressed too strongly. Therefore the campaign chairman must make a careful choice of the head of this group and of the other members.

In the smaller church the committee may be composed of the members of the Campaign Committee and a few others, perhaps the division generals. In the large church it should be a separate body of men who move in the same social, business, and professional circles as the prospects they call on.

Most of these larger contributions are pledged before the

formal opening of the canvass. The advance handling frees certain members of the group for other duties later. In addition these early gifts give some indication of how the effort is going.

Advance-gifts prospects are those who can give the bigger amounts. This includes most of the board members, many of the generals, captains, and team workers, and all the well-to-do people, whether in or out of the working organization.

The number of cards to be worked by this group will vary from church to church. In general it should be about 10 per cent of the card total. A good method is to withdraw from the campaign file all cards evaluated at five hundred dollars and up and lay them aside for advance gifts. If needed, some of the three hundred dollar cards can be added.

As these cards are withdrawn from the file, the corresponding cards in the office file are marked "advance gifts." Later when the cards are assigned to individuals, the advance-gifts worker's name is added to each office file card. A glance at the office file will show that the John Smith family is to be canvassed by Bill Jones, and Bill will be held responsible for the card until it is turned back with a report on his interview with the Smiths.

The amount to be raised by the advance-gifts group must be 50 per cent of the goal at the very least. It should be 60 per cent to insure success.

Taking again our fifty thousand dollar goal, we find that 60 per cent is thirty thousand dollars. The advance gifts group now has an objective of its own—thirty thousand dollars. If it's a three-hundred-family church, there will be about thirty cards—10 per cent—for advance gifts to work. This means thirty thousand dollars from thirty cards—or an average of one thousand dollars for each.

As the early reports begin to come in, the Campaign Committee will soon get some idea of how the canvass is going.

Of course this works out beautifully on paper. Would that it would do as well in the canvass! But it's better to get even a faint idea of how the wind is blowing than to remain in complete ignorance. After all, trends mean something in a campaign for money.

Distribution of big-gift cards to the committee members should be made at a meeting called as soon as the cards are ready and the brochure has been printed and mailed. The usual practice is to have the members choose the prospects they want to see. But the chairman should assign some of the cards to certain persons. It is important that some of those on the list be seen by the "right" people. About five cards is the right number for each worker.

A record is kept of those who take cards, as already mentioned; and the name of the solicitor is written on the corresponding card in the office file. The chairman must follow up closely on his group. He can't assume that the work is being done; he must know that it is. The chance for success depends on whether the committee does good work. If it doesn't, there's no chance at all.

Interviews with advance-gifts prospects must not be hurried. It's a mistake to approach a physician when his outer office is full of patients. Or an industrial executive when the union is asking a raise in wages.

Time and place are important. It may make a difference of many hundreds of dollars. The best place is the prospect's home, and the best time is in the evening or on Sunday afternoon. The next best place is over the lunch table. The right man can get an appointment over the telephone. But solicitation on the telephone? Never!

The good solicitor never tries to close the deal too quickly. Take time. Discuss the church and its program. Go over the pictures and sketches in the brochure. Be a good listener if the prospect will talk.

At the proper time mention what someone else has given —the pastor's pledge, if it represents real sacrifice, or the campaign chairman's. Set a high standard for this prospect. It's bound to affect his judgment.

He may ask for his evaluation. If he doesn't, tell him what it is. State that four other men (if this is the number) are being asked for the same, and ask: "Will you be one of five to pledge this amount?" This is the time to produce the card and have a fountain pen ready for action.

If the interview seems to be going sour, do not press the point. Ask the prospect to think it over for a few days. (In fact, experienced campaign directors advise two interviews with the bigger prospects.) The second contact may go better.

A word of caution to the campaign chairman: It's a well-understood principle in campaigning that a worker must be permitted to include his own pledge with his team report. If he isn't, he'll be just plain sore about it. He may not say anything, but he'll think a lot. What, then, shall be done about the signed cards of the captains and workers who are solicited by the advance-gifts group? The answer is to interview them just the same as anyone else but, after the card is signed, hand it back to the signer to report with his own team. This may pull down the advance-gifts total to some degree, but it's better than having any hurt feelings or ill will. The campaign chairman should explain this plan clearly to the group.

The Loyalty Dinner

Every event during the campaign is important, but there are three that stand out: the Loyalty Dinner, the Workers' Dinner, and the Campaign Sunday Luncheon.

The Loyalty Dinner is important because is signifies the formal opening of the preparatory period. It is held at the outset of the effort—soon after the decision to go ahead with the canvass. All members of the church are invited on a complimentary basis, and 70 to 80 per cent of them will come if the attendance is vigorously promoted.

The event is often held at a neighboring church or a hotel so that the women may hear the program rather than be busy with cooking and serving. It will cost more, but the expense is justified.

It is suggested that the Campaign Committee decide for itself that the meal will be free and announce it early. No one will object. If the question is thrown open for discussion at a board meeting or the like, someone will pop up and move that it be a paid affair; and no one will have the nerve to offer any objection. The motion maker may experience a thrill of pride, but the action will throw a measurable damper on the dinner attendance. Make it free, serve a good dinner, and beat the bushes to get everybody out. It may mean hundreds of additional dollars in the campaign coffers.

The Loyalty Dinner is for *information*. Although every effort may have been made to keep the congregation fully informed, many of the marginal members—the seldom-attenders—will have only the vaguest idea of what has been going on. By the time this program is over, every possible question that could arise in the mind of anyone should be answered.

What will the new building look like? How big will it be? The size of the sanctuary? How many can be seated? What building materials will be used? What will it cost? How will the money be raised?

If it's a modernization program: What changes will be made? Do we get a new kitchen? Where will it be located? Will we have a recreation room? Can the old classrooms be made over satisfactorily? Will these improvements answer our needs for years to come? And a thousand others.

The architect must be present to answer the questions that refer to the building operation. He should have sketches and drawings to be thrown on the screen or placed on easels. Cost estimates should be ready, since most people are cost-conscious in these days of high construction prices.

The Loyalty Dinner is also for *inspiration*. When the question about the method of raising the money comes up, the campaign chairman needs to put his best foot forward. Because of the informal atmosphere and satisfied appetites, this is his best chance to outline the campaign plans and put heart into his request for complete co-operation.

One good story from life, with a little sentiment in it, is worth a score of arguments. Here's one that was told at an event of this kind: A young couple, living in a rented house, with a moderate salaried income, had no car. They saved for many months and finally had $630 for a down payment on a used automobile. Then the church campaign for a new building came along. They were devoted to the church—but they wanted a car. Which should it be—the car or the church? No one knows how they may have wrestled with this question, nor by what process they arrived at a decision. But on the night that the first reports were handed in, the amount subscribed on their card was exactly $630.

The pastor will do well to dwell on the spirit that should prevail in the canvass—willingness, devotion, sacrifice. Apart from the money to be raised what are the spiritual gains that should come? To the workers? To the givers? To the children and young people? To the generations yet to be born?

If there's time, call on two or three ready speakers who will help things along by brief comments. But be sure they're brief. Avoid the garrulous old gentleman who will take up a half hour on the perilous state of world affairs. It's not the time or the place for a speech from a visiting senator or the appearance of a Hollywood celebrity. This is church business, and everything should be directed to the improvement program and the means by which it may be achieved. No outside person can help very much with this.

Avoid lengthy speeches and overlong sessions like the plague. The program should be timed, and participants should hold to the schedule.

It may be well to announce an early sacrificial gift, using the donor's name with his consent. The pledge should be large enough to set a high standard for others.

At the conclusion the chairman might make this parting request: "Many of you who are present tonight will be asked to work—as committee members, team leaders, campaign solicitors. Whatever it is, *please do not say 'no.'* We must not hear that word from anybody. It will be discouraging and defeating in its effect. What we must hear is, 'Yes, I'll do the best I can.' That will inspire all of us and help to generate the kind of team spirit that will win the game and achieve the victory." The chairman will find that an earnest appeal of this nature will cut down the number of refusals as the organization begins to be formed.

Prayer groups

The pastor and lay leaders will encourage the practice of prayer for the canvass—both before and throughout the duration. It might be well to announce a plan at the Loyalty Dinner, with details to be worked out by the pastor and a special committee. Here are four methods that have been used:

A *prayer league* involving the whole congregation may be formed. On the first Sunday after the Loyalty Dinner mimeographed cards are placed in the pews or handed to people at the Sunday services. A mere request that they be signed may not get a good response. A short talk on the importance of prayer should precede the request, and then enough time should be given for signing. The cards may be placed on the offering plates or taken home as reminders. This is a sample of one card that was used:

Believing in the power of prayer in the life of the church, I will pray daily from now to the completion of the building-fund campaign:
1. That God may guide and empower us in this project.
2. That everything may be done according to his will.
3. That the spirit of devotion and sacrifice may be increased in us all, so that we ourselves may become a large part of the answer to our prayer.
4. That we may enter into the joy of our Lord's commendation, "Well done!"

Signed _____

Date _____

If it seems desirable, the pastor might have these cards signed after his address at the Loyalty Dinner rather than on the following Sunday.

Home prayer meetings may be arranged. The city or community is divided into three or four sections, with a meeting scheduled for each of them at one of the homes. The sessions can be held on successive nights so that the pastor can attend all of them.

Some pastors are fearful that such meetings will not be well attended, and their fears are well grounded. Attendance must be "worked up," and there will be needed a committee for ways and means—such as announcements in the bulletin and from the pulpit, a letter from the committee or pastor to each family in the section, and personal telephone calls from the host or hostess to all church families in the neighborhood. Attendance is stressed so that as many as possible may be brought into the program, but the presence of even a half-dozen earnest people will make the event worth while.

The session should not be overly long—perhaps one hour. The program may center about some of the great promises in the Bible: Deut. 31:8, II Chron. 7:14, Mal. 3:10, Ps. 121:7,

Matt. 28:20, John 15:7, and the twenty-third psalm. Two or three devotional hymns might be used, and scripture reading, prayer, and a meditation by one of the group may complete the session. Or the pastor may lead a discussion on "How Prayer Can Help Us in This Canvass."

Church organizations may be asked to give a portion of their regular programs to sessions of guided prayer. The pastor or a special committee may provide a list of suggestions, such as the following:

1. That we may seek God's guidance in this program and that his kingdom may be extended in the hearts and lives of mankind.
2. That we may express our thanks for those who have labored in past years to build this church through their sacrificial gifts and works.
3. That God may guide and direct the leaders of this campaign and that everything may be done in accord with his will and purpose.
4. That there may be a spirit of willingness to serve on the part of those who are asked to assume any task in the campaign.
5. That every member and friend of the church may be moved to respond generously to the coming appeal.
6. That we may remember that our purpose is to see that every boy and girl, every young person and older person, may have a better opportunity for Christian training.
7. That the members of our group may be in prayer each day for the success of the canvass and that we may support the effort, under God's leading, by what we do and say and give during this great forward step on the part of our church.

Women's circles, service and missionary groups, and others have used this plan. Since they are already organized and hold regular meetings, there is no problem in promoting attendance.

An "upper room" club may meet with the pastor. Without publicity let him invite eight or ten carefully selected people for prayer sessions in his study two or three times in the weeks preceding the canvass.

Stewardship sermons

The pastor's influence will be far-reaching in his contacts with his parishioners—on the street, at the church building, in his study, and in the homes of the members. He should use every opportunity in personal interviews to spread the campaign gospel, <u>stressing particularly the spiritual emphasis that must be</u> at the heart of the movement.

But it is in his preaching that the best chance comes. He reaches many in the morning service whom he sees rarely at any other time. His earnest messages, Sunday after Sunday, should stir up some of the more unselfish instincts in his hearers and cause them to be responsive to the campaign appeal.

Some pastors may be reluctant to mention money from the pulpit. They shouldn't be. Jesus talked about money and possessions more than any other one thing.

The stewardship theme should be the paramount issue before the congregation at this time. The pastor will use his own best judgment in deciding how often and how hard he may keep pounding on it.

One pastor used this series of precampaign sermons:

We Would Be Building	Neh. 2:18
Foundations	I Cor. 3:11
Counting the Cost	Luke 14:28
Walls	Isa. 60:18
Inwrought Strength	Eph. 3:16
Unfinished, but Growing	Eph. 2:21
Furnishings	II Tim. 3:17

Other appropriate subjects are "Laborers Together with God," "Tools for the Task," and "The People Had a Mind to Work."

Publicity

The Publicity Committee has a busy time during the build-up period. As already described, it mails out two letters to the membership, the first of them enclosing an attractive informational brochure, and arranges to present audio-visual materials at whatever meetings of members can be arranged. In addition the committee must use every possible medium for telling its story to the congregation. Its responsibility is plain—to keep pounding on the campaign and the building project until they become the chief subjects of conversation and interest in every department of the church life.

Three-minute speeches can be used to keep up a veritable drumfire of facts and information before every adult and young-adult group in the church organization. This series of very short addresses should be given by competent laymen chosen from among the members. They address gatherings of every kind and description wherever a hearing can be arranged. Don't wait for invitations. Ask for permission to appear. The accent is on brevity. Short speeches do not wear out any welcomes; long ones are boring and ineffective. Don't be afraid of repetition. Why else would soap and toothpaste companies repeat the same old thing over and over again? They do it because it works. It will work with the church as well.

What is needed more than anything else, in addition to one or two briefly stated bits of information, is a convincing testimony of the speaker's favorable attitude toward the project. "I believe in this program. I believe in the campaign which will make it possible. I'm willing to pray for it earnestly, work for it zealously, and give to it generously." Nothing can beat personal testimony, as evidenced by patent-medicine vendors' constant use of the technique.

The church bulletin and paper during the weeks leading up to the canvass must be full of campaign information and inspiration. A paragraph or two should appear in every issue, and more when space can be arranged without crowding out announcements of the regular church program.

Newspapers, radio, and television are usually available for some general publicity about the campaign. The amount of space or time depends on the size of the community. Since it is likely to be rather limited in any case, the schedule for the reports needs to be chosen so that they will do the most good. However, keep in mind that these general news reports will not raise money. They merely let the public know that your church is alive and building for the future.

Newspaper copy must have news value if it is to get by the city editor. The job can best be handled by someone who can write good copy and knows his way around in the newspaper offices. Papers will give space to stories before the canvass and to reports of the money raised at the end. They will use architects' sketches of the new or remodeled building and pictures of the pastor and campaign chairman. Sometimes, when they have room, they will print the names of the leaders and workers.

Radio and television stations will probably mention the campaign at two or three significant stages if reports of it can be fitted into their regular broadcasts of local news. The reports must be "news" and must state the facts in only two or three sentences. In smaller towns stations may be willing to broadcast an interview with the pastor or campaign chairman and even air several spot announcements on a public-service basis.

Young people should be brought into the undertaking in some manner, both as a matter of information about the project and as a stimulus to future leadership on their own part. They do not go out on assigned calls ordinarily under the age of twenty, unless with an experienced canvasser who will handle the interview.

One good method is to announce a poster contest bearing on the purpose of the campaign. The posters can be either serious or humorous. Hang them on the walls of the Sunday school assembly rooms and other conspicuous places in the building. Then move them to the dining room on the night of the Workers' Dinner. The winner might receive a prize or some special honor at that time.

A slogan contest is another suggestion. Young people sometimes come up with some highly interesting ideas.

Timing the publicity for greatest effectiveness calls for careful planning. The congregation must be subjected to an almost continuous barrage of publicity beginning with the invitations to the Loyalty Dinner and building up to a climax as the active canvassing starts. The Publicity Committee should work out a complete schedule, selecting the strategic release date for each item and then figuring out the steps in its preparation so that everything will be ready to make its impact at the psychological moment.

The Solicitors 5

Visiting every member family in the congregation to se-cure its pledge to the building fund is a job that calls for an efficiently organized and carefully instructed corps of so-licitors. Many of those who have already served on commit-tees will want to take part in the actual solicitation. In ad-dition to these there must be selected the most enthusiastic members of the congregation to make up the working organi-zation. Every one of them should be thoroughly dedicated to the task. If there are any active members of the church who show a spirit of opposition or even disinterest toward the project, they should be kept busy with other assignments and left out of the group of solicitors, for they will do more harm than good.

The size of the working organization is geared to the num-ber of families in the membership. One worker is needed for every five families. This means that each pair of workers, go-ing two by two, will have about ten families to cover, includ-ing their own.

Take a church of three hundred families: About 30 cards—roughly 10 per cent—have been withdrawn for advance gifts. This leaves 270 cards for the general solicitation. With 5 cards assigned per worker, fifty-four workers will be needed.

Divisions and teams

For efficient organization the workers should be formed into teams of six or thereabouts. Each team is led by a captain—or, better still, a pair of cocaptains. If there are as many as six teams, then the teams should be grouped into divisions, each division having from three to five teams. Each division is headed by a general.

Take the church of three hundred families again: The fifty-four workers will make nine teams of six workers each. The nine teams will best divide into three divisions of three teams each. Figure 9 shows a chart of this organization.

Of course a smaller church needs fewer workers and therefore simpler organization. For example, a congregation of one hundred families calls for only eighteen workers divided into three teams, no divisions being necessary.

Selecting the solicitors is a process that calls for proper handling. There will be more enthusiastic co-operation throughout if the leaders are allowed to choose those who will work with them. But there will be confusion and wasted time if they are simply turned loose to recruit workers without any co-ordination. The more popular and better-known members will be besieged from all sides, and other good prospects may be overlooked. So some sort of plan like the following is needed to assure that only one approach will be made to any one person.

As soon as the division generals are signed up, they are called together; and the whole campaign plan is explained to them by the campaign chairman. They then select their prospective captains from an alphabetical list of suggested leaders prepared by the Campaign Committee with the advice of the pastor. Of course any general is free to suggest additional names, but it saves time to have a good working list prepared in advance. Figure 10 shows an example of such a list.

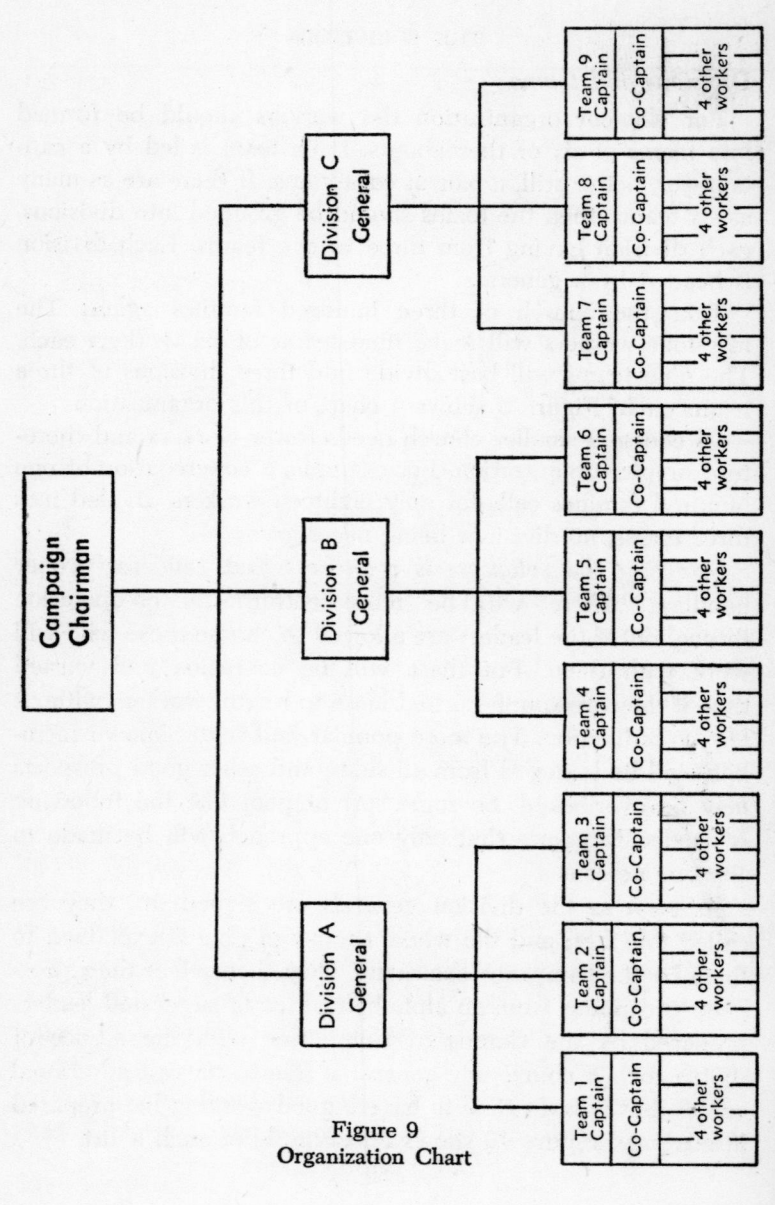

Figure 9
Organization Chart

Prospects for Captains	
1. Mr. and Mrs. Harold B. Brown	11. Mr. and Mrs. Henry J. Schlundt
2. Mr. and Mrs. Eddie Edwards	12. Mr. and Mrs. William M. Smith
3. Mr. and Mrs. Clarence Deeg	
4. Mr. and Mrs. Blake Foster	13. Mr. and Mrs. Courtney Smith
5. Max Lewis, Jr.	14. Mr. and Mrs. Rolland Sheafor
6. John Lewis	15. Mr. and Mrs. J. Ervin Taylor
7. Jim Little	16. Mike Taylor
8. Woody Little	17. Mr. and Mrs. Bish Thompson
9. Mr. and Mrs. S. J. Medlicott	18. Mr. and Mrs. Gale Weedman
10. Mr. and Mrs. Carlton Sexson	19. Mr. and Mrs. Joseph G. Wick
	20. Mr. and Mrs. Don Wood

Figure 10
Prospective Captain's List

A copy of the list is placed before each general, and he is asked to check a half-dozen names he would like as captains in his division. It will save time later for each general to have his choices marked so he can state them promptly. As soon as all are ready, the general of Division A announces his choice of a man and wife, or two single names, for cocaptains of one team and puts his initials after their names. Each other general draws a line through those names. The general of Division B then announces a choice, followed by the other generals in turn. As each name is chosen by some general, the others cross it off their list. After all have announced one selection, let the last general choose again and reverse the order, so as to equalize the advantage of first choice. Go back and forth until each general has nearly twice as many as he will need —to allow for refusals. Keep a master list, showing all names chosen and by whom.

The generals should be asked to call on their prospective captains immediately and report those who accept. A time is set for the captains to meet. It can be five days later, or a week if there is plenty of time.

It is a good thing to send a letter of thanks to each pair of captains as the names are reported, and urge attendance at the captains' meeting.

Much the same procedure is followed at the captains' meeting. After an explanation of the campaign plan longer lists of suggested workers are handed out, and the cocaptains take turns choosing names till they have enough to be sure of securing the four additional workers they need for their teams.

The duties of captains need to be very clearly explained so that all will know what they are expected to do. To forestall any misunderstanding, hand out a mimeographed summary of the responsibilities, such as the following:

1. Line up enough workers quickly from the list you have chosen to make up a team of six.

2. Report to the church office promptly the names of those who will serve.

3. As soon as your team is complete, release the names of any you have not approached. Some other captain may need them.

4. See that the members of your team are present at the Workers' Dinner and the Campaign Sunday Luncheon.

5. Let your team members choose their assignments from the cards allotted to your team and see that they sign receipts for them so that you and the church office will know who is responsible for each prospect.

6. Supervise the work of each team member during the canvass and see that he works all his cards.

7. If any team member cannot cover all his assignments, secure someone else to complete them for him.

8. At each report meeting collect the pledges and cash contributions from the team members and turn them in with a combined report for your team.

Note that women have been included, both as captains and as workers, in these suggestions about organization. They are good campaigners and are often more faithful than the men. Some campaign directors use only men for canvassing, reserving the women for hostess and hospitality work at the campaign events—on the theory that women carry more than their share of the general church program and that this is a good job for the men. However, the plan of having man and wife as cocaptains as recommended here works too well to pass up. They can work together in lining up their team members, and one or the other can always be present at meetings to represent the group.

As the organization proceeds, the secretary should set up a team chart in the office, adding the names of workers as they are reported.

A letter of thanks from the campaign chairman to all who have accepted responsibility of any kind is always in good order. It promotes interest and reliability.

Making up card assignments

The operation of dividing the cards among the teams is quite simple if an orderly process is adopted and carried through step by step. If it is done haphazardly, however, the end result will be utter confusion, with a disastrous failure to get full coverage. In plain terms this means a material loss of income to the church.

Several good methods of making up card assignments have been used. The one favored here is the "geographical plan," whereby the city or community is divided up into sections, with each of them to be canvassed by a single unit of the working group. This saves time and gasoline, and gives the members of each team a compact and clearly defined part of the total coverage in which all their work will be done. As developed in the following pages it still leaves with the team members their own choice of the prospects who live within the boundaries of the section which has been assigned to the team. This choice is made in team meetings at the conclusion of the Workers' Dinner.

To see how it works out in detail, let us use again the three-hundred-family church previously mentioned. In this case we have three divisions, with three teams on each one, to work 270 cards after 30 have been withdrawn for advance gifts. Here are the steps:

1. Take nine envelopes, of any convenient size that will hold the pledge cards. Type on each one the team number and the captains' names for one team. Each of these envelopes will hold the cards to be worked by one team.

2. Withdraw from the campaign file the personal cards of all the workers on the teams (remembering that some of the workers' cards are already in the hands of the Advance Gifts Committee) and put each worker's own card in the envelope of the team of which he is a member. This is done so that each team may work the cards of its own members and receive credit for the pledges made.

3. Divide the city or community into three sections, using a map if one is available, and separate the cards by their addresses into these three sections, shifting a few around until all three have about the same number. Each of these sections is the assignment for a division.

4. Now take the cards in Division A and separate them geographically into three small groups in the same manner, equalizing the numbers. Put each packet in one of the envelopes marked for Teams 1, 2, and 3, adding it to the workers' cards already there. Then place these three small envelopes in a larger one and mark it Division A. Repeat this for Divisions B and C.

There are now three large envelopes, each of them containing the cards to be worked by one division. With more or less divisions and teams the operation will vary accordingly.

It is probable that a number of rural addresses will be found. These are always hard to locate, since only route and box numbers are given. If the office records contain any directions for finding these residences, the secretary should copy them on the backs of the cards. As for those about which nothing is known, the best way is to assign an equal number to each team and place on the workers the responsibility for finding them. The pastor can usually help with this problem, and names read at one of the report meetings will sometimes bring the information.

The Workers' Dinner

The Workers' Dinner is scheduled for the Thursday or Friday night preceding Campaign Sunday, when active solicitation by the team workers is to begin. Every effort must be made to insure the attendance of every team worker, as well as the advance-gifts group and every committee member in the organization. This event is for everybody who has any part in the canvass, and experience shows that few who miss this program will do effective work.

The following measures may be used to promote attendance:

1. Announcements in every committee meeting and church group for two or three weeks before.

2. A personal appeal from the pulpit on the preceding Sunday.

3. A letter from the campaign chairman to each worker a few days before the dinner, thanking him for his promise to serve, with a strong invitation to be present.

4. A call by the Telephone Committee to each worker on the day before the dinner. This can be done on the legitimate

plea that the Dinner Committee must know how many meals to prepare.

5. Putting it up to the captains to get their own workers out.

6. Announcement that the dinner will be free in spite of the high cost of living. It is a proper item of expense to be charged against the campaign budget.

On the morning of the dinner the office secretary must see that the arrangement of the dining tables is explained to the building custodian, unless this responsibility has been given to the Decorating Committee. A long table, or a series of tables, should be placed for each division of workers, so that the teams in that division can be seated in numerical order along the sides. After the tables are set, the place cards are stood up in their proper locations. The secretary must lay a worker's kit at each place, including the head table at one end. In one corner of the dining room there should be an additional small table, loaded with extra pledge cards, brochures, card receipts, clips, rubber bands, and pencils.

Several hosts and hostesses should be appointed to arrive early and greet people as they enter the dining room. As the crowd gathers, they usher the pastor, campaign chairman, and other leaders to the head table and help team members find their assigned places.

The Dinner Committee should see to it that there is enough help to serve quickly when the teams are seated and to remove the dishes as soon as possible after all have eaten, that kitchen noise is not allowed to interfere with the program, and that outside dishwashers are hired so that the cooks and servers from the membership can come in for the session.

The campaign chairman presides over this event, and he should hold closely to a time schedule so that workers will not be slipping out the door if the hour grows late. Like the Loyalty Dinner, this is not a time for long speeches from anyone. Keep the program spirited and interesting from the first moment to the last. Here are a few suggested items for the program:

1. Singing, with a good song leader to infuse spirit and enthusiasm into the group.

2. A brief dramatic or humorous skit bearing on the canvass, given by a group of young people under experienced direction.

3. A five-minute discussion by the chairman on "The How and Why of the Canvass."

4. A sound movie on "How to Canvass."

5. A short address by the pastor on "The Spiritual Aspects of the Campaign."

6. A one-minute challenge by each division general, pointing out why his division will lead all others in the campaign.

7. An explanation of "The Mechanics of the Campaign" by the chairman or someone experienced in selling. This is the time for the training session, described in the next section of this chapter.

8. An interview demonstration with a prospect, showing both right and wrong methods of soliciting. A good deal of humor may be introduced. This should follow the training session and point up some of the principles which have been stated.

9. A period of earnest prayer for God's blessing on the enterprise.

This is a good time for a sacrificial gift or two to be announced, even if this has been done at the Loyalty Dinner. It will help to set a high standard of giving and end the program on an optimistic note. A telegram announcing a generous contribution by someone who is absent from the city might be arranged.

It is not intended that all the features mentioned will be used in one meeting. The session would be too long. Short team meetings will follow the program, and time for them must be allowed.

Training the solicitors

The usual time for the training session is at the Workers' Dinner. An evening meeting or two for this purpose may be held previously, if desired, when there will be more time; but the attendance will not be as good.

The mechanics of the canvass should first be made clear to all the workers, with the whole procedure outlined in detail. They need to understand how the pledge cards are to be filled out for weekly and monthly payments and also for any other methods of payment that prospects may prefer, and must be prepared to answer any questions about plans for payment. The method of distributing the boxes of envelopes is explained at this time so that the workers may pass the information on to the contributors—or distribute the envelopes themselves if this is the method to be used.

The workers are told that they are to visit in pairs, since it has been found that this method is usually more productive. Insurance representatives and other salesmen may prefer to go alone, but even if one person does most of the talking, an inexperienced partner may learn something by going along—and often may help by talking to the wife while the more experienced worker bears down on the husband, or vice versa. Each worker will choose five cards, so the two who work together will be responsible for a total of ten prospects, including themselves.

The best hours for soliciting will be from one to four on the afternoon of Campaign Sunday, when people will still feel the inspiration of the morning worship. The workers should be urged to make the most of their opportunities during this period. Thereafter the calls will have to be completed on Sunday evening and the following evenings of the week, when folks who were away from home during the afternoon may be found. For these calls after dark a flashlight to see house numbers is almost a necessity. When no one is in at the first visit, a business card or penciled note left in the door may suggest that another call will be made the next evening. Some prospects work on an evening shift or for some other reason are rarely home at the usual visiting hours. The worker may be able to reach such a prospect by telephone in the morning and make a date to call in person at a convenient time.

The schedule for the report meetings should be emphasized, and the procedure for turning in pledges, cash, and information to the captains should be made clear. Brief reports on prospects who do not pledge are needed so that the Campaign Committee may judge whether or not to make another try on them. Also the church office needs reports about changes of address and about illness and other situations calling for pastoral attention.

After explaining these mechanics of the canvass, give time for questions. Several workers are likely to ask about points that many need to know.

Principles of good canvassing should then be presented by someone who can handle the assignment—an insurance representative or a teacher of salesmanship. A few "do's" and "don'ts" are helpful to those who have had little experience in this kind of work. Here are some suggestions:

1. See every prospect *in person*. A telephone solicitation seldom secures a satisfactory pledge.

2. Before approaching the house, note the evaluation on the back of the card and remember it. Keep the card in your pocket until the prospect is ready to sign.

3. Conduct the interview *inside* the house, not from the front porch. The query, "May we come in for a few minutes?" will bring an invitation to enter.

4. Spend from fifteen to twenty minutes with the prospect. Take time. Workers are in the business of making friends for the church as well as getting pledges for money.

5. Use the brochure to turn the conversation to church matters. Avoid any early reference to pledging. This comes later. Refer to one of the pictures or sketches. Comment on the improvement program in prospect. Invite questions and discussion. This may lead up to the moment when the prospect inquires about his evaluation or when the amount may be mentioned by the solicitor. The card may then be produced, with an earnest plea for a generous contribution. If the evaluation is for five dollars a week, for instance, and the "standard of giving" in the brochure shows that five such gifts are needed, the all-important question will be, "Will you be one of five to pledge five dollars a week?"

Occasionally a person will ask what he should give. A definite answer must be ready, using the evaluation amount. If he asks what others are pledging, mention a few of the more substantial amounts.

It must be remembered that many will have clearly in mind what they intend to give, and they want no advice from anyone on the question. The team worker needs a kind of sixth sense to know how hard he should press for a definite figure.

6. A prospect sometimes states that he owes on a previous pledge and wishes to clear it up before signing another. The best solution is to include the delinquent amount in a new pledge, even if it is only the unpaid arrearage. The pledge then becomes current, and there is a better chance of collecting it. If the prospect is informed that the pledge will count on the campaign objective, he will be more amenable to the suggestion.

7. If the prospect refuses on the basis that he doesn't believe in signing pledges, tactfully accept this as a conscientious

conviction. A statement that he made a pledge when he was married, bought property, or opened a charge account would only start an argument. If he will agree to accept a box of envelopes and will name an amount which he will try to give each week or each month, it may properly be included in the canvass report if his giving record has been good.

8. Prepare for each individual interview. It should not be entered into in a careless or haphazard manner. Get two or three main appeals clearly in mind. There may be no chance to use them, but have them ready if an opening comes.

9. When the pledge has been made, whether large or small, thank the signer for his help. This is a good time to press for church attendance if he hasn't been going.

10. Avoid taking cash if it can be done. But if the prospect insists on paying cash, or if a cash payment is made on account, sign the receipt stub on the pledge card and leave it with the contributor. The cash or check should be clipped to the card to avoid mistakes in the office.

11. If there is a refusal to pledge, note the fact on the card and hand it back to the team captain. Every card must be turned in so that the office may know that the prospect has been seen.

12. At some addresses there may be more prospects than those listed—relatives of the family or roomers. After getting the main pledge, inquire if there are any other church members in the house. It may be profitable to canvass these folks, using the extra pledge cards supplied in the kit.

13. After every interview leave the prospect with a mutual feeling of good will, even if there has been a refusal. He may change his mind later.

14. Don't leave the card with the prospect on his promise to "think it over" or "talk with my wife." His agreement to mail it in will usually not be kept. Rather, keep the card and make a date for a later call.

15. Don't argue with the prospect about anything. This is vitally important. Arguing can do no good and is likely to do harm. It's best to listen quietly to complaints and criticisms, and then get the interview back on the track. If there is a legitimate grievance, pass it along privately to the proper church official.

16. Finally—don't be scared! Canvassers are not mendicants, and they have every reason to be proud of the thing they're doing. Only once in a blue moon do they have unpleasant experiences, and then it's usually because they allow themselves to be drawn into arguments. On the contrary they'll be thrilled by many of the contacts they make.

For example, on one occasion, just as the workers were leaving for their first calls, a young man said to me, "I'm scared of this thing. They've told me how it should be done, but I'm still scared. I've never asked anyone for money, and I don't know how to begin. But I promised to work, and I'll do the best I can."

That evening, as he turned in an excellent report, he told what had happened.

"My first call," he said, "was on an old lady who lives alone and makes her living by cleaning houses. When I walked up on the porch, she opened the door before I had a chance to ring the bell. She was smiling up at me, with a pledge for fifty dollars, already made out, in her hand. She said, 'Frank, I've made this out for fifty dollars, but I want to give sixty if you'll help me get a little more cleaning work with some of the church families. I haven't any children, but other people have. They need this new building, and I want to see it go up!'

"After talking with her for a few minutes," Frank continued, "I thanked her for her pledge—which was away over and beyond what she should have given—and left. As I walked down from the porch, my eyes were so full of tears that I could hardly see my way. But my chin was out, and my shoulders were back. I was ready to face anything. If I'd met the devil on the street, I would have asked him for money for the church."

There may not be time to cover all sixteen points carefully. Some of them may be passed over quickly, but others should be given emphasis. It is recommended that the office secretary prepare mimeographed copies of the more important points to be handed out after the presentation is over.

A few words should be said about television if it is available in the community, for it creates a problem for the canvasser. If he interrupts a program, he may not be received as cordially as he would be otherwise. An amateur Hawkshaw may be on the point of pinning the murder on someone in the case, and the family wants to know who it will be. What should the canvasser do about it? Here are a few answers from actual canvassers:

"When I can see from the porch that a program is in progress, I slip away quietly and come back later. It takes more time, but I believe it to be a better plan."

"If I know the people well enough, I ask them if they would mind turning off the program for a few minutes while I explain my call." Question: Is this the right atmosphere for an interview, and does it give time enough?

"I knock at the door and ask quickly for a definite appointment for a day or two later."

This question needs to be explored by the Campaign Committee, so that some counsel can be given on the best course to follow under the conditions that exist in the community.

Distributing the Cards

At the conclusion of the Workers' Dinner the prospect cards which have been prepared by the office secretary are distributed to the workers. Even if the training session has been conducted previously, the cards should still be held back and given out at this time.

The large envelopes, described earlier in this chapter, are handed to the generals, who in turn give to the captains the small envelopes inside. The cards in the envelopes will be chosen by the workers at the team meetings to follow.

There is still one thing to be done before the large group breaks up into team sessions. The campaign chairman must appeal to all workers to sign their individual pledges before they leave the building—or at least before the solicitation begins on Sunday. They should do this because:

1. It will be an example to others.

2. It will set a high standard of giving.

3. No team member can conscientiously ask another to give until he has signed his own pledge.

This is the time for a last appeal for all workers to cover their cards and "do it now." A final word might be a reminder of how well the prospects have been prepared by the letters and brochure which have gone out to all members. There should be a cordial reception in every home. The chairman will also wish to announce the Campaign Sunday Luncheon again and press for a full attendance. He may then dismiss the workers to their team meetings.

The team members gather in separate groups around the table or in other parts of the building. They should have their workers' kits with them. There are three things for them to do in these meetings:

1. Choose the cards they want as the captain reads the names.

2. Sign card receipts for the cards they accept.

3. Sign their own pledges and hand them to the captain to be turned in at the first report meeting.

Each captain must see that all card receipts for his team are filled out and handed to the office secretary. This information will be transferred to the corresponding cards in the office file not later than the next day. The Campaign Committee will then know who has which card and whether it is being worked as the campaign proceeds. This is part of the plan to secure complete coverage on all prospects.

Campaign
Week   6

*A*ll that has happened up to this point, with the exception of the advance-gifts solicitation, has been but a prelude to what will happen now. Plans have been made, committees have been at work, materials have been prepared, teams have been organized, and workers have been trained in the principles of good solicitation. But all depends on the work of this week, and the pattern will be set on the very first day—the Big Day—Campaign Sunday.

The general solicitation starts this afternoon and will continue throughout the week. The second Sunday night will see most of the work done, but there may be mop-up calls to make later until every prospect has been seen.

This is an important and far-reaching period in the life of the church. What is done and said and given during these eight days will have a significant bearing on the future of the congregation for a score and more of years.

The Sunday morning service

The thought of the worship service on Campaign Sunday will naturally center on the canvass. A suitable text for the sermon may be found in Gen. 28:22. Other references are I Kings 5:5 and Neh. 2:18.

If the pastor has not stressed tithing previously, this would be a good time for it. Certainly the church with a fair number of tithers has few financial troubles. And it's a good system for the participant as well as the church. It gives him an added sense of obligation and encourages the spirit of stewardship.

A loyal churchman once told me, "My wife persuaded me to start tithing, and I've been doing it for several months. When I get my check and selling commission each Saturday, I put down one tenth of the amount in my account book. That is reserved for the church. There are three things about this practice that I have noted and for which I have no explanation: I give more easily and cheerfully than I gave before. I give more than I gave before. And I seem to have more left." Perhaps the explanation of the apparent paradox may be found in Mal. 3:10, Luke 6:38, or Mark 10:21.

"Proportional giving" is another system in the practice of stewardship by which the member agrees to set aside a definite per cent of his income—5 per cent, for instance—for religious causes. This may lead to tithing later.

Time should be given at this service for the campaign chairman to explain the general plan for solicitation and to ask for the wholehearted support of the congregation. He may ask the members with the exception of the team workers, to remain in their homes until four o'clock. On the other hand he should state that there are more calls than can be made in a single afternoon and that some of those present may not be reached until later in the week. Certainly he will urge that every team worker remain for the luncheon to follow the morning service, and announce that the childrens' room will be open for use as long as it may be needed.

The Campaign Sunday Luncheon

This luncheon should be held soon after the morning service.

To conserve work and expense, it can be a sandwich and coffee affair. Perhaps the people will work better if they are not too well fed.

Why have the luncheon? Why not go home for dinner and leave from there? There are two good reasons:

1. The average worker would go home and eat a big dinner, take a nap, listen to the radio, and put off the dreaded hour until much later in the afternoon. The luncheon plan gets everybody on the streets by one o'clock. Any later hour would find many prospects out in their cars if the weather is fine. The luncheon saves an hour or two of precious time.

2. Many of the workers are timid about the job before them. If they can enjoy a session of good fellowship around the tables and then leave in a body, they gain an added sense of sharing in a common task which is beneficial to all of them.

The place cards should be in position and the teams arranged in the same manner as at the Workers' Dinner. The office secretary should have the several kinds of supplies ready in case of need.

This is a time for last-minute questions and discussion. A brief review of the "do's" and "don'ts" of good canvassing might be made.

Decide on the few points that need most emphasis and speak of these last. For example, a reminder to remember on approaching each house to memorize the family's name and the evaluation on the back of the card, and then pause in a moment of prayer, a conscious reaching out for divine guidance. Finally the team members should be urged again to follow through on every card and to report back the results of their afternoon interviews at the designated hour that evening.

After a brief devotional period all should leave quickly for their assignments.

Report meetings

After the luncheon the tables should be put away except for three or four which will be needed by the captains in making up their reports, and the room should be prepared for the first report meeting that night. The office secretary sees that pencils are supplied, also clips and rubber bands. The thermometer is in place, together with a brush and a can of red paint. Someone who can do good lettering is ready to mark up the scoreboard. A small adding machine aids in figuring division totals and the grand total when all reports are in, and someone is appointed to operate it. The secretary stands ready to collect each envelope as soon as it is reported.

The schedule of meetings needs to be planned early enough to be mimeographed in the instructions to the workers, as already mentioned. Sunday, Wednesday, Friday, and the following Sunday nights are usually the best. If stores are open on Friday nights, requiring the presence of a number of the workers, or there is some other conflict, schedule the midweek report meetings for Tuesday and Thursday.

The best hour for the report meetings is eight o'clock. If there is a Sunday-evening service or a midweek service, set the session to follow it, with an invitation to the worshipers to attend and hear the reports.

The second Sunday night should see the greater part of the cards finished, perhaps all of them. If a number remain unworked, a meeting should be set for the following Sunday night. If the workers are followed up closely, the job can be cleaned up by that time.

Captains should come early to the report meetings, both to greet their team members and to make up their report envelopes. Accuracy in copying card numbers and amounts will save the Audit committee a lot of grief.

The reporting by captains is of course the feature of these meetings. Call on each captain as soon as he is ready, disregarding the order in which names appear on the scoreboard. Some will be slow because of the late arrival of certain team members. Each report should be applauded, whether large or small.

In addition to his pledged amount ask each captain how many cards were assigned to his team, how many he is turning in as completed, and how many are yet to be worked. Have a small blackboard at one side where these figures can be displayed. If this is done at each meeting, it will be a strong spur to the team members to finish all their cards.

After the third meeting, on Thursday or Friday night, the office secretary should make up a list for each captain which will show the unworked cards still held by his team members. The alert captain can then check the list with his workers and exact a promise that the job will be completed by Sunday night.

A complete list of the same unworked cards should be made up for the campaign chairman. He can read the list on the second Sunday night and ask which of the prospects have been seen and the cards handed in, and which remain unworked. Those who haven't finished their work should state in public that the rest of the prospects will be seen without fail by the following Sunday. If they are not willing to make this statement, they should hand over their cards and let someone else take care of them.

If there has been a good solicitation job, there should not be many cards left after this fourth report meeting on the second Sunday night. If there are a few, the office secretary should make up another list for each captain on Monday morning. This contains the names on the unworked cards which were originally assigned to his team. Opposite each name appears the name of the team worker who is responsible for the card.

The captain must follow through on these cards during the week. This is another method of keeping up the pressure until the task is done. There should be a complete coverage by the next Sunday night.

Encouraging the workers is a function of the report meetings that is even more important than securing the figures of what they have accomplished. A spirit of enthusiasm and optimism and group morale must be kept up at each session.

The figures on the scoreboard are of course a tremendous stimulus to further work. Those who have good reports take pride in seeing the record of their success and are eager to do it again. Those who have run into difficulties see the success of others and realize their own future efforts will turn out better. Those who have loafed a bit see how they are letting down their fellow members and determine to give their best for the remaining drive.

There is a problem about this, however, at the meeting on Tuesday or Wednesday evening. On leaving the church Sunday following the luncheon most of the workers will have hurried at once to their most promising prospects. These pledges plus their own will have added up to a beautiful report on Sunday night. But since then the going will not have been so easy. The figures to be added at the second report meeting will probably look rather sorry by comparison, and they may discourage the workers.

To meet this situation, some experienced campaign directors believe it a good policy to hold back several large advance gifts and work them into the report meetings when they will do the most good. If it appears that the new figures for the second session will look slim, these large amounts may be tossed in to bolster the total and infuse new life into the group. If the prospects look pretty good on Tuesday or Wednesday anyway, some of these big amounts may be reserved even for Thursday or Friday.

On the other hand other directors prefer to report all pledges, including the advance gifts, at the earliest meeting of workers possible. They believe that the greater stimulus comes from close approach to the goal. Certainly it is true that, with only a few thousands left to go, workers can reach a high pitch of zeal for getting every additional dollar to bring them nearer to going over the top.

This is where the thermometer comes in. It is a climactic moment at every report meeting when the total amount is added up and the red stripe can be painted a few inches higher toward the top. Call on the pastor's wife, the chairman's wife, or some other prominent lady to mount the stepladder and apply the paint—and give her rousing applause for her artistry.

Praise for good work is a fine thing for every worker. There are two deeply ingrained instincts in human beings: they want to be recognized and appreciated, and they want to feel important. The successful sales manager knows all about these characteristics and uses them. The campaign chairman must do the same. It always pays. Better work will be done.

Watch for any outstanding bit of work. Have the member stand up and get a pretty girl to pin a rose on him. Compliment the captain whose team finishes all the cards first or brings in the greatest number of pledges or the biggest pledged amount. Honor the winning division at each meeting. Be liberal with praise wherever it can honestly be given.

On the other hand refrain from faultfinding, even when things are not going too well. The figures on the board which show the small number of cards worked by any nonfunctioning team tell the story. It's up there for everybody to see, and the captain, if he has any pride at all, will get his team members working before the time of the next meeting.

The spirits of the group should be kept at top level by all practicable means. It's possible to have fun even while raising money, and an amusing stunt or two each night can be a morale builder. One hilarious bit of nonsense has been used many times: present a pie to the winning team and bring in a collection of long-handled spoons, butcher knives, potato mashers, and whatnot from the kitchen for the workers to use in place of silver.

Analyzing the returns

As soon as the first reports are in, the campaign chairman, with the help of the office secretary, should begin a running analysis of returns—to be continued throughout the week. This analysis should ordinarily cover only the general canvass, since the advance gifts are not typical. It should show the following items:

1. The percentage of pledges secured from cards worked thus far—the cards worked being the total of those turned back by the workers, whether with pledges on them or with reports of refusal, removal from the city, decease, and so on.

2. The average amount pledged.

3. An estimate of returns to be expected from unworked cards if they follow the same percentage and average. This estimate must be recognized as too high, because of the fact that the better cards, with few exceptions, are worked first.

4. The ratio of pledges to evaluation—that is, the total of pledged amounts received thus far divided by the total of the evaluations on these same cards. If the original evaluation total was twice the goal, then the ratio of pledges to evaluations at every stage should be about one half (assuming the Evaluations Committee did its job reasonably well). This is really a better guide to what is happening than the estimate above, as it allows for the tendency of the workers to visit the better prospects first.

Along with this analysis the secretary should turn over to the chairman the cards that have been turned back with reports of refusals. A review of these may yield a number worth recanvassing and may also reveal some recurring objection or misunderstanding which the workers should be instructed how to meet.

The Campaign Committee should meet a time or two during the week to study the analysis and the refusals and discuss with the chairman the trends that are appearing. These must be considered along with the advance-gifts returns, which are already known. If advance gifts have been above the average required, a slight letdown in pledges from the general membership is not serious. If both groups are above average, there is cause for rejoicing. But if they are both below, the outlook is not so good.

Emergency measures are called for if the trends show the pledges are not meeting expectations, and the committee must act at once. Here are several things that can be done:

1. Press for group contributions—from the men's class, the women's class, the young married folks' group, the youth organizations, and others. The appeal should reach the group presidents in time so that action may be taken at the Sunday-morning sessions. Possibly they should be warned previously that such a request would be made in case of need. Since this is a real crisis in the life of the church, the payment of a substantial amount can be a legitimate class project during the coming year. In some cases several thousand dollars have been raised in this manner.

2. Recanvass board members and top leaders for increases.

3. Make a select list of advance-gifts contributors to whom another approach may be made. Send the "right" people to see them.

4. Pick a few of the refusals where another visit will have some chance of success. An emergency may bring about a change of attitude.

5. There's one other measure which I hesitate to mention, for it should not be used except in dire necessity. It is for the pastor to state in public that he will increase his pledge by an appreciable amount in order to reach the goal. This sacrifice should stimulate a similar response all along the line. But don't use the method if it can possibly be avoided. The pastor's income and his family responsibilities are the determining factors. He only can be the judge.

If despite all efforts the goal is not topped, don't give up. Announce that the campaign will be continued for three months and keep up a barrage of publicity during this time. Include a paragraph in each copy of the bulletin and church paper which will show the campaign standing from week to week. Play up all additions to the total for all they are worth. A letter or two to the membership near the close of the period may bring in some last-minute money that had not been anticipated.

A Victory Dinner, or at least a dessert affair, seems a well-deserved reward when the workers complete their task. How about planning one for the closing Sunday night? Some committees have stated in their precampaign publicity that such an event would be held and have given the date. Such faith is admirable, without doubt. Yet it is a fact that some campaigns do fail, and a Victory Dinner without a victory falls a little flat. Better withhold any such statement until the committee is sure of the outcome.

If, however, there is good reason to expect a victory by the time of the last report meeting, some kind of celebration may well be planned as a closing event. It will be a time of rejoicing and jollification, a happy ending to a hard job, and the beginning of a new and challenging period in the life of the church.

The Follow-up 7

After a successful closing, there will be big sighs of relief all over the place—from the pastor, the campaign chairman, and every other member of the working organization. But the work is not yet done. There must be letters that will acknowledge the service given by committee members and team workers, and also the gifts of the contributors. A system of records and collections must be set up and an adequate amount of insurance protection provided for the property from the moment construction begins. Further, an appraisal and report on the campaign operation should be prepared for presentation to the congregation.

Letters of thanks and confirmation

Remembering that everyone likes to be recognized and appreciated, the campaign chairman and the pastor should send a joint letter of thanks to all persons who have served in any capacity in the effort.

Equally important is a letter to every contributor, noting at the bottom the total amount pledged, cash payment if any, and the remaining balance. This serves as a confirmation of the pledge if no protests are received within a reasonable time.

On account of the number to be sent, the letter may be mimeographed by the office secretary and signed personally or with a stylus. Since mistakes are sometimes made, it is suggested that after an expression of warm thanks the concluding paragraph be something like this:

The figures shown below are taken from the church records. If there is any mistake about them or if they are not according to your understanding, please let us know, and correction will be made at once.

Amount of Subscription	$_____
Amount Paid	$_____
Balance	$_____

The figures can be filled in with pen or typewriter. The statement may save some hurt feelings if by any chance a contributor hasn't been credited with a cash payment or his pledge has been listed incorrectly.

Records, collections, and insurance

Now that the canvass is over, there are three necessary measures to be taken to conserve the results of the effort: (1) good records, (2) a well-planned follow-up on collections, and (3) adequate insurance coverage. It's too hard to raise money to allow it to slip away by poor business methods or the risk of a fire loss after the building is started.

The Campaign Committee should give consideration to a system of records and collections very early. Don't leave it until solicitation begins. Insurance protection will be needed before any construction is done.

Records of the building fund must include a ledger system of some kind to show the pledge of each contributor and to provide a place for crediting payments as they come in. The treasurer may wish to set up his own plan, or he may order loose-leaf forms and binders from the church supply house.

These are available to cover both building fund and current budget accounts if desired, or as a separate accounting system in case a special building-fund treasurer is appointed, as is frequently done.

The treasurer should be bonded and should be required to present a monthly statement on collections to the church board. Also it will encourage regular payments from the members if information on receipts is included in the bulletin and church paper from time to time.

To facilitate good records, special building-fund envelopes are required. Ordering and distributing these have already been discussed. An extra supply of them, undated, to put in the containers on the backs of the pews is advisable to provide for members who forget to bring their own.

Collections are the point of the whole campaign and must not be neglected. Most of the pledges will be paid promptly and regularly. There will be a few that become delinquent though, and these should be given attention before they get too far behind. It's a ticklish job and must be handled carefully. Any sort of cold, printed statement showing that the member is in arrears will result in resentment and ill feeling. Business concerns may get away with this, but churches can't. Yet this is not to say that delinquent accounts should not be followed up closely. They must be, for the member who is allowed to get further and further in arrears is likely to let things slide and quit altogether.

The cause of slow payment may be unemployment, illness, or a death in the family. In time of trouble no man appreciates what he regards as a "dunning" letter from his church. The circumstances should be known before an approach is made. They may indicate the course to be followed. Perhaps it's a friendly letter which will first thank the member for his pledge and then ask whether the payment is too big and should be reduced. Better still is a personal visit from a tactful board member. If there is trouble, he will soon learn what it is and know what to do. Perhaps the delinquent account should not be mentioned at all—or the member may bring it up. In any event it's better to lose the entire amount than to antagonize the member.

There are some people in most churches who are consistently late in paying what they owe. They may be careless about such obligations or just plain stingy. Whatever the reason, it will take frequent letters, telephone calls, and personal visits to keep such members fairly well up to date.

A strange type is the man, fortunately not too common, who becomes known for his generous pledges to many good causes and then never pays anything on any of them. He may as well be written off and forgotten.

So that the collection problem will not be neglected, it is recommended that a small committee go over the accounts from time to time and decide on what is to be done.

This group can judge whether the collection system is working well by an estimate of the rate at which payments are being made. Suppose the campaign has brought in $35,000 in cash and one-year pledges. The cash during the canvass has amounted to $5,000, leaving $30,000 for the next twelve months—or an average of $2,500 monthly. If there is a slight lag in meeting this monthly average over the next several months, it is not too serious, since a little pressure near the close of the twelve-month period will bring up the slack. If, however, there is a big drop over the first five or six months, an analysis is needed to determine the cause so that corrective steps may be taken.

Insurance protection is not a direct factor in a building-fund campaign, but it becomes one immediately afterward—or just as soon as construction begins. And if more churches were properly insured, there would be less need for finance campaigns. Consider the following figures: In a single recent year there were 3,200 church fires in the United Statees, with a loss of $9,000,000. A detailed study of church fires over a period of ten years shows that 39 per cent of the loss had to be borne by the parishioners. Without a doubt much of this was caused by neglect on the part of the church officials. These facts should bring home to church people the absolute necessity of a thorough study of their insurance needs, with a re-examination every year or two. Here are several specific points to keep in mind.

1. Builders' risk insurance is needed to take care of the building while it is in process of construction. When the work is done, the unexpired portion of the premium cost may be applied to the permanent policy.

2. Expert counsel should be sought on the right amount of coverage on the completed building. It is foolish to over-insure when the same protection can be had for less. And it is grossly negligent to underinsure and so subject the congregation to the danger of a heavy loss.

For example, a new building costing $100,000 is insured for the full value on a flat-rate basis. In the next few years the cost of labor and materials drops 20 per cent. Figuring in depreciation, the structure is now worth about $75,000. This is the amount which the insurance companies will pay in case of a complete loss—not the $100,000 which the church has been carrying. The premium payments on $25,000 have been wasted. The insurance committee should have reduced the coverage in line with falling costs.

But suppose the costs go up 20 per cent during these years. The cash value is now $120,000, less depreciation. It is now underinsured, and more protection is needed.

3. The burden of proof is on the policyholder in case of a fire loss. Put away in a fireproof safe somewhere should be

full information on the original cost of the building, together with a complete inventory of the furniture and fixtures, with the date of purchase and initial cost.

4. Every few years an appraisal of the building and contents should be made by someone whose estimates will be recognized by the claim adjustor's office. This is of special importance when insurance is written on the coinsurance basis.

5. If a coinsurance policy is written, it should be understood. If it's an 80-per-cent policy, for instance, the church must maintain coverage to the extent of 80 per cent of the insurable value of the property. If it doesn't, it is in trouble in case of fire.

Here's an example. A church building is worth $50,000 according to the appraisal. It is stated in the policy that 80 per cent of this figure—$40,000—must be carried in insurance. Suppose the church through negligence carries only $20,000. This is but half the amount which it agreed to carry, so in case of a fire the company will pay only half the loss.

Coinsurance is quite legitimate and is used by many churches and other institutions. But its provisions should be thoroughly understood.

In some states coinsurance can be written on the parsonage along with the church building. In others the flat rate must be paid.

6. To sum it up: Deal with a good insurance man who knows his business. Consult him frequently in times of changing values. Read the policies and understand them. Maintain an up-to-date inventory of the furniture and other equipment. And get an appraisal of the property from time to time.

Every church building, no matter how old, is a monument to the sacrifices of generations now gone. The work of years may be destroyed in a few hours. It's a sacred trust which no church official can afford to avoid or neglect.

Appraisal and report

Someone has stated that a task is not completed until it is recorded. With a building-fund campaign the job isn't done until an analysis is made of the methods of operation and of the financial outcome. Further, there is need for an evaluation of the spiritual effects of the undertaking on the leaders, the workers, and the membership in general.

The Campaign Committee should make such a study soon after the closing date and present a summary of its findings to the congregation. Even although the church does not envisage another canvass in the near future, the time may come when such an appraisal will be of immense value as other building projects are in prospect.

The campaign operation might be judged by considering such questions as: What were the strong and weak points in the planning and supervising of the campaign? In the building of the organization? In its form? In the evaluation of the prospect cards? In the publicity? In the handling of supplies and materials? In the training and encouragement of the solicitors? In report meetings? Was there complete coverage of the cards? If not, what was the reason? Were the pledges accurately recorded and an efficient collection system set up?

The financial outcome is of course the easiest thing to determine. Was the goal reached? How many pledges were made? What percentage of the church families subscribed? What was the average contribution? How did the pledges compare with the evaluations?

Regarding the spiritual effects, any realistic measurement is difficult; but some appreciation of what has happened in the congregation may be gained by an examination of the following questions: Is there evidence of a new spirit of stewardship among some of the members? Do their contributions represent real sacrifice, as nearly as this can be judged? Has there been a discovery of new leadership? Is there an awareness that the new building is only a means to the end that the spiritual needs of the members may be met and a program of Christian service carried on? Have some lukewarm members been brought into active fellowship? Are the members united in support of the bigger and more far-reaching program ahead?

A successful campaign should result in a deepening and quickening of the spiritual life of the congregation, a greater appreciation of the responsibilities of church memberhip, a keener sense of the stewardship of talent as well as money, and an increased devotion to both the local and the world mission of the church. It is an inestimable privilege to have a part in these achievements.

INDEX